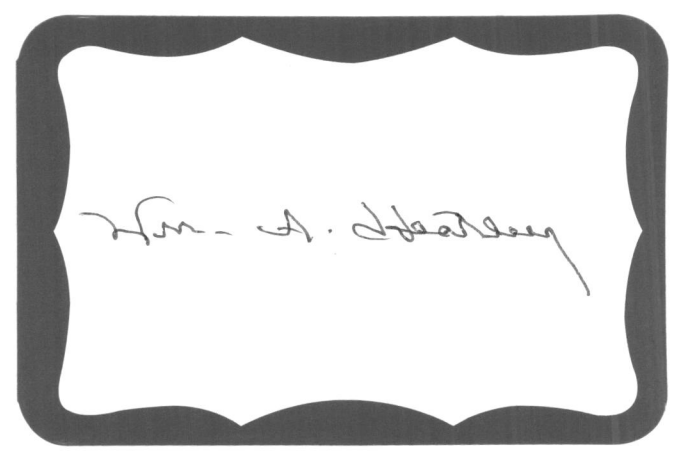

PRIVATE HOUSES OF FRANCE

Christina Vervitsioti-Missoffe

Text Christiane de Nicolay-Mazery
Photography Francis Hammond

PRIVATE HOUSES OF FRANCE
Living with History

Flammarion

Simultaneously published in French as
Grandes demeures françaises, traditions d'élégance.
© Flammarion SA, Paris, 2014

English-language edition
© Flammarion SA, Paris, 2014

All rights reserved. No part of this publication may be reproduced in any form or by any means, electronic, photocopy, information retrieval system, or otherwise, without written permission from Flammarion S.A.

Flammarion S.A.
87, quai Panhard et Levassor
75647 Paris Cedex 13

editions.flammarion.com
styleetdesign-flammarion.com

Dépôt légal: 10/2014
14 15 16   3 2 1
ISBN: 978-2-08-020164-5

PAGE 2 *The enfilade at the Hôtel Lambert.*
ABOVE *Detail of one of Jean-Baptiste Oudry's paintings for the dining room at the Château de Condé.*

EXECUTIVE EDITOR
Suzanne Tise-Isoré
Style & Design Collection

EDITORIAL COORDINATION
Frédérique Popet

EDITORIAL ASSISTANTS
Sarah Rozelle and Lucie Lurton

GRAPHIC DESIGN
Bernard Lagacé

TRANSLATED FROM THE FRENCH BY
Barbara Mellor

COPYEDITING
Helen Downey

PROOFREADING
Sarah Kane

PRODUCTION
Élodie Conjat

COLOR SEPARATION
Les Artisans du Regard, Paris

PRINTED BY
Tien Wah Press, Singapore

8 CHÂTEAU D'ANET
RENAISSANCE JEWEL

50 CONSTANCE AND HER LITERARY SALON

68 COUNTRY LIFE AT CHAMPCHEVRIER

98 A DAY AT THE HUNT AT CHAMPCHEVRIER

124 DISCOVERIES AT THE CHÂTEAU DE CONDÉ

148 CHILDHOOD MEMORIES OF PRINCESSE G.

162 THE ELEGANCE OF HUBERT DE GIVENCHY

190 AN AMERICAN IN PARIS

206 ANCESTRAL TREASURES IN PARC MONCEAU

218 ROMANTICISM AND NOSTALGIA AT MONTRÉSOR

242 FAMILY MEMORIES IN THE MARAIS

266 LUNCH WITH ALEXIS DE REDÉ

LEFT *The author, Christiane de Nicolay-Mazery, at the Château de Champchevrier.*

French style may have its roots deep in the sweeping tide of history, and it may often derive its glory from a distinguished past, but the style that is revealed in these pages is also enriched with a sense of personal intimacy and of family lives lived. It is these private touches, just as much as the more grandiose vestiges of history, that help to create a magical "spirit of place," and to imbue a house with a soul. It is these personal elements that anchor these homes firmly in the reality of the here and now, and that fill them with life in the world of today.

The interiors that make up this fresh portrait of this inimitably French *art de vivre* are largely historic, and some of them boast immensely long pedigrees—but none of the owners who have agreed to throw open the doors of their homes is inclined to look backward, none of them tends to focus on the past. On the contrary, they all live to the full in their own century. They have all developed their own personal style, unique to themselves, and they have all created their own world—their own realm—in their own image.

A home is a whole world, made up not only of memories and of real life, but also of plans for the future, of enthusiasms, and of passions. As the philosopher Gaston Bachelard put it, a home is not merely a dwelling place, but also, and more importantly, a "dreaming place."

Each of the owners of the châteaux and *hôtels particuliers* visited in these pages enjoys an intense and intimate relationship with their home—occasionally, as with Alexis de Redé and the Hôtel Lambert, bordering on obsession. Through their home, each of them is pursuing an ideal of some sort, a dream that they are determined to bring to life.

For some of them, as at Anet, at Champchevrier, or at Montrésor, the challenge lies first and foremost in taking over the reins of an ancestral home—of enhancing its beauties, of restoring it where needed, and of breathing life into it. I am thinking, for instance, of the joy and pride felt by the successors of the lovely Diane de Poitiers at the Château d'Anet, as they contemplate their success—centuries after her death—in restoring the château and its gardens to their former splendor and magnificence.

For others, as at the Château de Condé, it all began with a vision: the dream of waking a beautiful château from its long slumbers, of revealing its memories, and discovering its secrets. Adventures of this sort are often punctuated with wonderful surprises, such as the recent discoveries at Condé of a painting that may be by Watteau, and of a little door hidden behind layers of wallpaper and topped with a painting by Lancret.

And for others still, their first meeting with the place that would be their home was a veritable *coup de foudre*. When he first saw the Hôtel Lambert on the Île Saint-Louis, Alexis de Redé was captivated and enthralled, vowing that he would never leave it: "My life has been transformed, this is where I want to live!" He had found the nostalgic haven of beauty that he had yearned to rediscover since childhood, and now he would devote himself to transforming it into a magical, timeless palace.

Whether we are exploring the private spaces of Hubert de Givenchy's *hôtel particulier* in Paris, roaming through the salons of the Princesse de Salm-Dyck on rue du Bac, gazing on the astounding painted decorations at the Château de Condé, or discovering the more intimate world of an artist friend in the Marais, the beauty of these places never ceases to astonish and enchant us—offering a healing balm not only for the eyes but also for the soul.

For all these reasons, I offer my heartfelt thanks to all those friends who have so generously opened the doors of these great French private houses, allowing us to share their pleasure at the feats they have accomplished, and their enjoyment of the unrivaled beauties of homes that embody to perfection all the elegance of French style.

LEFT *Lady at her Toilet*, School of Fontainebleau, c.1560.
FACING PAGE *The ceremonial entrance hall offers a dazzling introduction to one of the finest jewels of French architecture, the setting for the clandestine romance between the lovely Diane de Poitiers and Henri II. The superb staircase with its graceful single flight sets the tone for the magnificence that speaks of Anet's royal past, and of the romantic story of its heroine, Diane de Poitiers.*

CHÂTEAU D'ANET
RENAISSANCE JEWEL

PHŒBO SACRATA EST A[
VERUM ACCEPTA CUI

E DOMUS AMPLA DIANÆ
UNCTA DIANA REFERT

The Château d'Anet—a Renaissance masterpiece built where Normandy meets the Île-de-France for Henri II's favorite, Diane de Poitiers—invites us to take a romantic excursion through history. Following in the enchanted footsteps of the lovely Diane, we can only marvel at the elegant restraint and flawless style of the château and its grounds, while musing on the memories of royal passions, the vagaries of time, and the vicissitudes of fate in which its walls and gardens are steeped. From the moment we step into its magnificent entrance hall, we become aware that Anet's history is inextricably bound up with the passions of those who lived here.

Two buildings stood on this site before the present château: the original medieval fortress was demolished in the fourteenth century, to be replaced in the fifteenth by a brick-and-stone manor house, gifted to Pierre de Brézé by Charles VII. This was the property that Louis de Brézé inherited in 1490, on the death of his father Jacques. In 1515, at the age of fifty-six, he married Diane de Poitiers, who was then just fifteen. Lord of Anet and Grand Sénéchal of Normandy, Louis was one of the important men in the kingdom. He was also Grand Veneur de France (grand master of the French hunt) and François I and his courtiers came regularly to hunt on his lands.

The young Diane played an enthusiastic part in these hunting expeditions, having accompanied her father's hunting exploits— with her own falcon—from the age of six. Hunting was her passion—portraits often depicted her as Diana the huntress—and there was nothing she loved more than a long day in the saddle followed by a bracing cold bath.

When Louis died in 1531, his young widow mourned him sincerely. Adopting widows' weeds, she was to wear only black and white for the rest of her life—though always in the most sumptuous of fabrics, adorned with rich jewels and cut with plunging décolletages. She now lived at court, where she was a lady-in-waiting to the queen.

By this time Diane was thirty-two and a dazzling beauty, to whom François I's second son, the future Henri II, developed a passionate attachment while only in his teens. Even marriage to Catherine de' Medici did little to cool his ardor. In 1538, when he was not yet twenty, Diane became his mistress. Henri too now wore her monochrome colors, and adopted the famous monogram composed of their interlaced initials, "H" and "D", henceforward to be seen everywhere.

In 1547, Diane decided to build a new château at Anet. She entrusted the drawing up of the plans to the architect Philibert Delorme, who designed a central building to house apartments for herself and the king, flanked by two wings enclosing an entrance courtyard, reached through richly decorated gates. By 1552 the work was complete. The interior, embellished with painted coffered ceilings and magnificent furniture bearing Diane's monogram, was of unprecedented splendor. Its fame spread immediately, and one glittering party succeeded another there. The king and his entire court flocked to the celebrations and entertainments laid on by Diane. In the grounds, exotic birds fluttered overhead, while tame cheetahs prowled the parterres. But this indulgent, carefree life was to prove short-lived. Barely six years later fate was to put an end to the fairy-tale, when Henri II was killed during a tournament. Diane de Poitiers was to remain at Anet until her death in 1566, ever beautiful, ever mysterious.

After her death, Anet passed through the hands of a long list of the distinguished and powerful. First was Louis-Joseph, Maréchal de Vendôme, the great-grandson of Henri IV and Gabrielle d'Estrées, who added the great entrance hall and the wrought-iron stair balustrade bearing his monogram, and who brought in Le Nôtre to design the gardens. This outstanding soldier, who fought in every one of Louis XIV's campaigns, indulged in a life

PAGES 10–11 *Reclining above the entrance doors is a copy of Benvenuto Cellini's* Nymph of Fontainebleau; *the original is now in the Louvre.*
FACING PAGE *The monumental entrance portal is topped by a clock with moving bronze figures: originally the stag would tap its hoof and the two dogs would bark silently to mark the passing of the hours.*
PAGES 14–15 *The château viewed from the gardens.*

of luxury and dissipation at Anet, where he received the Grand Dauphin and hosted spectacular events of all kinds, including games, banquets, and wolf hunts. The estate then passed to the Duc du Maine, the legitimized son of Louis XIV and Madame de Montespan. When the Revolution broke out, the château was one of the residences of the Duc de Penthièvre, grand admiral of France, who was highly respected for his charitable works, and was left undisturbed by the Revolutionaries.

After his death in 1793, by contrast, a long period of ruin and devastation awaited the château, which was caught up in a storm of upheavals. The family's possessions were confiscated for the nation, and the estate was placed under sequestration. In 1794, the furniture was auctioned off. In June 1795, the tomb of Diane de Poitiers was desecrated, her coffin forced open and her remains thrown into a common grave. In 1798 the estate was divided into lots and sold off, and the château was stripped bare.

In 1797, Alexandre Lenoir, founder of the Musée des Monuments Français, had arranged for the state to buy a number of scattered fragments of Diane de Poitiers's tomb, as well as the *Nymph of Fontainebleau* by Benvenuto Cellini, which Philibert Delorme had placed above the main gateway, and the *Fountain of Diana*—so saving these masterpieces from destruction. This did not deter the château's new owner from demolishing the central part of the château and its right wing in 1804. Of Philibert Delorme's original design there now remained only the left wing, the monumental entrance portal, and the sublime chapel.

In 1820, the Duc de Penthièvre's daughter managed to regain possession of the now abandoned estate, before selling it on to the Caraman family. Not until 1860 was the château finally rescued from oblivion, when it was bought by a Paris stockbroker, Ferdinand Moreau. This ancestor of today's owners set about literally saving the château and putting it back together, scouring the region for traces of its glorious past, and tracking down the decorative features, paneling, painted fragments, and furniture that had once embellished it. He even managed to unearth Diane de Poitiers's bed, which had ended up in a village inn, and her sarcophagus, which was being used as a pig trough. With doggedness and persistence, he was determined to restore life and elegance to this former royal residence. On Moreau's death, his son-in-law Guy de Leusse inherited Anet. In 1944, he in turn bequeathed the estate to his granddaughter Laurette de Leusse, who with her husband Charles de Yturbe continued the major works of renovation and restoration. Today, their son Jean de Yturbe and his wife Sandy—worthy heirs to the spirit of this unique place—devote themselves with equally fervent passion and immaculate taste to ensuring that Anet remains one of the most remarkable of all French châteaux.

Nowadays it is easy to imagine Diane de Poitiers riding across the parkland and along the canal, dismounting to enter the magnificent gilded entrance hall and cross the vast red salon to reach her bedchamber, its bed hung with sumptuous gold embroideries. There she would rediscover all the luxury and refinement she so loved in her own era, the magnificence she so prized, as well as the cloaked intimacy of her royal love nest. If the beautiful Diane de Poitiers were to return to her estate today, she would surely be astonished by its recaptured splendor.

PAGES 16–17 *The entrance hall.*
FACING PAGE *Detail of a carved wooden door bearing the monogram of Louis-Joseph, Maréchal de Vendôme.*
RIGHT AND PAGES 20–21 *A pair of seventeenth-century halberdiers, their halberds forming torchères, flank the doors leading to the great red salon, where the ceiling displays the coats of arms of all the château's owners down the centuries.*

IT WAS HER CUSTOM EVERY MORNING, THEY SAY, TO TAKE POTIONS OF GOLD. BRANTÔME, *Mémoires du Seigneur de Brantôme*

BELOW *The paneling in Diane de Poitiers's bedchamber, which is decorated with her emblem, the crescent moon and the royal "H". The graceful paintings on the door panels recall her love of horseriding and hunting, as well as depicting the falcon she was given by her father at the age of six.*

FACING PAGE *Diane's boudoir, in one of the château turrets. Frequently depicted "at her toilette," the celebrated beauty probably hastened her death in 1566 by her habit of drinking a gold elixir each morning in order to preserve her translucent complexion. Vaunted at the French court for its "marvelous properties," liquid gold was in fact poisonous.*

YET I LOVE A LIFE
OF POETRY AND RAPTURE,
IMMORTAL TREASURE
IN A SETTING LOVELY TO BEHOLD;
FOR MY ECSTASIES I LOVE
THE FLASH OF RUBY, TOPAZ,
AND CHRYSOPRASE,
OF HEAPS OF SILVER AND OF GOLD!

THÉODORE DE BANVILLE, *Reprise de La Dame*

PAGES 24 AND 25 *Diane de Poitiers's bed, miraculously discovered in the nineteenth century in a village inn.*
LEFT AND ABOVE *A pair of silver-gilt wedding chalices and a detail of an inlaid ivory box.*
FACING PAGE *The fireplace in the large dining room is decorated with telamons by the sculptor Pierre Puget. They show the influence of the ships' figureheads for which he was famous. The sixteenth-century silver nef on the table is mounted on a tray with casters, on which condiments and wine would be placed.*

FACING PAGE *Set of engraved glasses.*
BELOW *Detail of the sumptuous marquetry floor in the small dining room, featuring Diane de Poitiers' crescent moon emblem.*

CHÂTEAU D'ANET: RENAISSANCE JEWEL 29

IN THE SIXTEENTH CENTURY, DIANE DE POITIERS CREATED A LIBRARY THAT WAS CONSIDERED AMONG THE MOST REMARKABLE OF ALL RENAISSANCE LIBRARIES.

FACING PAGE, ABOVE, AND RIGHT *The walls of the passage leading to the library are hung with a collection of engravings depicting the Château d'Anet at the time of its construction, which began in 1547 and ended in 1552. The architect Philibert Delorme designed a building consisting of a central block flanked by two wings enclosing a walled entrance courtyard. Today only the left wing of the château survives.* BELOW *The black-and-white photograph shows Isabelle, Philippe, and Jean de Yturbe (the present owner, on the left).*

CHÂTEAU D'ANET: RENAISSANCE JEWEL

PAGES 32–33, LEFT, ABOVE, AND FACING PAGE *The prints salon, also known as the family salon, is decorated with architectural drawings depicting the construction of the château. Jean de Yturbe and his wife Sandy, the present owners, have transformed this royal residence into a large family home, filled with life. This black-and-white photograph shows them with their daughter Diane.*

MADAME CHARLES DE YTURBE, NÉE LAURETTE DE LEUSSE, INHERITED ANET IN 1944 AND RESTORED IT TO ITS FORMER SPLENDOR AND ELEGANCE.

FACING PAGE *One of the guest rooms.*
ABOVE *View of the chapel at Anet.*
RIGHT *The lady in the blue cape painted by Jean-Claude Fourneau c.1948 is Jean de Yturbe's mother, Madame Charles de Yturbe, née Laurette de Leusse. After inheriting the château in 1944, she and her husband embarked on a major program of refurbishment.*
PAGES 38 AND 39 *A charming bathroom decorated with flowered wallpaper. All the bathrooms are furnished with faience* nécessaires de toilette *marked "Anet."*

BELOW AND FACING PAGE *A little corridor flooded with light leads to another guest room containing a Louis XVI canopy bed hung with a Braquenié fabric. If Diane de Poitiers were to return today, she would discover the same elegance, splendor, and faultless taste as the château boasted in her own day.*

A BIRD AWAKES, FLUTTERS ITS WINGS, AND FLIES.
A WINGED FLOWER BLOOMS IN THE MORNING LIGHT
IN THE GENTLE BREEZE, AMID BLUSHING SKIES.
LECONTE DE LISLE, *Dans l'Air Léger*

ABOVE AND FACING PAGE *A tiny boudoir in one of the turrets, complete with a delicate antique mirror and window overlooking the gardens, encapsulates the special charm of Anet. A delightful chinoiserie wallpaper, featuring little figures swinging from branches, others using mushrooms as parasols, and squirrels nibbling hazelnuts, decorates another guest room.*

THE KING AND HIS COURT FLOCKED TO THE ENTERTAINMENTS LAID ON BY DIANE. IN THE GROUNDS, EXOTIC BIRDS FLUTTERED OVERHEAD, WHILE TAME CHEETAHS PROWLED THE PARTERRES.

BELOW AND FACING PAGE *A small door let into the oak carriage entrance to the* cour d'honneur *allows a glimpse of the magnificent surrounding parkland. The vast grounds at Anet, originally laid out by Le Nôtre, were transformed by the Bühler brothers into an English-style landscape park in the nineteenth century.*

NEARLY 450 YEARS AFTER HER DEATH, DIANE DE POITIERS HAS BEEN LAID TO REST IN HER CHAPEL AT LAST.

PAGES 46 AND 47 *The chapel at Anet, a Renaissance jewel, was completed by Philibert Delorme in 1550. The interlocking circles of the coffering in the dome form a flamboyant trompe l'oeil design creating the illusion of a great cupola. The design is echoed in the fine marble pavement, the dome and pavement together forming a circular design of dizzying intricacy.*

FACING PAGE AND ABOVE *The more modest funerary chapel of Diane de Poitiers, consecrated in 1577, features a central statue of Diane kneeling at prayer. In 1793, Revolutionaries desecrated her sarcophagus and flung her remains into a common grave. In 2008, DNA taken from a lock of her hair preserved in a medallion was compared with bones removed from the common grave. The results of the tests confirmed that bones taken from the upper part of the grave were indeed Diane's. They are now preserved in a small sarcophagus in the funerary chapel. Nearly 450 years after her death, Diane de Poitiers has been returned to her rightful resting place.*

FACING PAGE *Joseph zu Salm-Reifferscheidt-Dyck—friend of Jussieu and Alexander von Humboldt and a passionate botanist, reputed to have possessed one of the finest plant collections of his era—bought this handsome hôtel particulier in the Faubourg-Saint-Germain in 1809 for his wife, Constance de Théis, so that she could realize her dream of holding a literary and artistic salon. This well-regarded early nineteenth-century salon was frequented by men of letters, painters, scholars, and musicians. It was in this library, known as the music room, that Constance used to receive her guests.*
LEFT *Detail of the ceiling painting by Antoine Vaudoyer.*

CONSTANCE
AND HER
LITERARY SALON

FACING PAGE *Detail of a door and internal shutters, painted with delicate motifs in a soft palette of grays and pinks.*
PAGES 54-55 *Under the Empire and the Restoration, Constance gathered a glittering company in her salon: scholars such as Prony, Jussieu and Redouté, artists including Cherubini, Talma and Girodet, and writers such as the young Alexandre Dumas.*

An inventory drawn up in 1780 offers a glimpse of the elegance of this residence at the end of the Ancien Régime, when it was known as the Hôtel de Ségur. It describes the residence's magnificent grand staircase "with its steps in *pierre de liais* limestone," its two antechambers opening on to a "formal apartment" of three rooms *en enfilade*, and on the left a perpendicular wing housing more rooms, "one paved in stone, the others with parquet floors."

During the Revolution, houses abandoned by émigré aristocrats were not merely sequestered but also pillaged and looted. This was the unhappy fate of the former Hôtel de Ségur, which amid all the upheavals was left abandoned, a mere shell open to the elements, dilapidated, ravaged, and stripped of every stick of furniture. When the turmoil died down, the prospective buyers of this disaster zone lingered long enough only to gauge the scale of the work that would be necessary. In around 1800, however, Joseph zu Salm-Reifferscheidt-Dyck, a German prince, passionate botanist, and horticulturalist, had the happy idea of buying it, believing that, once refurbished and decorated, in the fashionable taste, the reception rooms would make the perfect setting for the artistic and literary salon of which his wife dreamed.

This lady, born Constance de Théis, was a French poet greatly admired by men of letters for her presence and beauty: Stendhal praised her bosom, Benjamin Constant her arms. While well aware of the power of her looks, Constance preferred to be recognized for her talent—she had had some success with poems published in the *Almanach des Muses* when she was eighteen—and for her reputation as a woman of letters at the heart of the artistic life of her era. The mansion, now renamed the Hôtel de Salm-Dyck, rose from its ashes to play a prominent part in the intellectual life of the period, becoming a much-frequented literary salon, which in its elegance and success could bear comparison with those of Constance's great role models, Madame Récamier and Madame de Staël.

Minor though it may be, Constance's contribution to literary history was not wholly unworthy of the literary circles that she admired with such a passion. While the tragedy that made her reputation, *Sapho* of 1794, with music by Martini, is now forgotten along with most of her poetry and other writings, her epistolary novella, *Vingt-quatre heures d'une femme sensible* (A Day in the Life of a Woman of Sensibility), which she kept secret for over ten years before she published it, justify her place—modest but warranted—in the literary pantheon.

Every Paris salon had its own rules, its own policies and protocol. No prominent members of the imperial staff would be found there, with the exception of Barbier, librarian to Napoleon. Nor were there any swaggering military types or braggarts. The salon's habitués fell into three categories: scholars such as Prony, Jussieu, and Humboldt; artists including Houdon, Vernet, Girodet, and Cherubini; and writers, from Paul-Louis Courier, to whom Constance was very close, to the young Alexandre Dumas. While widely varied in their talents and personalities, they all shared one common characteristic: all of them were already, or would later be, figures of great distinction. Of the thirty-nine members who regularly climbed the elegant main staircase, seventeen were already or would soon become members of the Institut.

But times change, and—*mutatis mutandis*—places that were once the height of fashion are soon overtaken by new addresses, new places in which to be seen. As Louis XVIII was succeeded by Charles X, in 1824, the "New Athens" bordered by rue Blanche, rue La Bruyère, and rue Saint-Lazare attracted artists of the Romantic movement that was now in vogue to the Right Bank, abandoning the Faubourg-Saint-Germain. And in order to keep up with the latest fashion, the Salms too

crossed the river, leaving behind them the lovely residence that they had brought back to life.

Nearly two centuries later, the *hôtel particulier* has been restored to its former glory and splendor. The art-lovers who now live here have restored the original colors of the magnificent painted ceilings to wonderful effect. Each of the two salons that essentially formed the original formal apartment has its own particular charm. The gray-and-gold palette of the ceiling in the salon known as the drawing room, painted in relief and featuring a remarkable octagonal frieze representing the four elements alternating with the muses, the arts, the sciences, and the military arts, lends the room a masculine air.

The other salon, known as the music room, is softer and more feminine in feel. The sprightly palette of the ceiling, the birds flitting between the garlands of flowers, and the swans with outstretched wings at every *écoinçon* all reflect the delicate tastes of Constance de Salm. Two pairs of double doors, each topped with a basket of fruit evoking one of the four seasons, give access to this charming space, which still seems to hum with society chatter.

The authorship of the remarkable painted ceilings in the formal apartments has been debated for many years. Until recently, the presence of Girodet among the Salms' inner circle, and the similarities with some of the decorative schemes carried out at the Hôtel de Beauharnais under his direction, prompted specialists in the field to attribute all the decorations to him. But in 1980, a discovery was made at the Musée des Arts Décoratifs: a set of watercolors was unearthed by the architect Antoine Vaudoyer, who was also part of the Salm set. Among them were dated and signed paintings of the two ceilings. The attribution of the ceilings to Vaudoyer now seems beyond doubt—although the possibility that the artist Jean-Jacques Lagrenée, another regular visitor, also contributed to them still remains open.

The soft light of the Faubourg, filtering through the shutters and casting a gentle glow on the oak parquet and leather bookbindings in the library, sets me daydreaming. I imagine the lovely Constance leading one of her regular guests to the majestic staircase. To whom has she granted her favors today: Cherubini, Talma, Alexandre Dumas? Like a jealously guarded secret, the Hôtel de Salm-Dyck preserves the private memories of this literary salon that was her dream, and that, for the space of a few years, brought her glory.

LEFT *An elaborate gilt bronze window latch decorated with the "S" of the Salm family and a swan.*
FACING PAGE *Guests who signed Constance's visitors' book left behind them watercolors, poems, snatches of music, and portrait sketches. Every member of her brilliant salon was devoted to an art, a passion, or an ideal.*

les connaissances et la bonté sont d'une femme les plus grands ornemens.

Paris 20 avril 1810

Les qualités sociales sont très estimées à la chine; les reunir au plus haut degré est inutile pour une femme pour lui faire obtenir de l'empereur l'ordre que le souvenir en soit conservé par un monument. imitons ce louable usage, et n'écoutant que la voix et l'opinion generale, écrivons ces mots chinois. 得 se 撒 sa 黙 me, 衆 tchong 意 y. {Je-same, est le nom chinois de madame la Comtesse de Salm y Tchong y me, l'opinion generale a consacré ce monument.

litteralement; En l'honneur de celle qui possède et répand la sérénité, l'opinion générale a consacré ce monument.

POETRY SHOULD BE THE EARTHLY MIRROR OF THE DIVINE, REFLECTING IN ITS TONES, MUSIC, AND RHYTHMS ALL THE BEAUTY OF THE UNIVERSE. GERMAINE DE STAËL, *De l'Allemagne*

PAGES 58–59 *The lovely painted ceiling of the music room, by the architect Antoine Vaudoyer, whose other projects were to include the extension of the Collège de France and the Sorbonne. Viewed from below, the Empire chandelier forms a rosette in the center of a neoclassical painted décor of swans and lyres against a sky-blue cornice, with birds flitting between garlands of flowers.*
ABOVE *A portrait of Constance by Joseph Marie Vien the Younger from the visitors' book, and a watercolor depicting Pegasus by Carle Vernet.*
FACING PAGE *Handsome leather bindings in the library.*

ON THE SKY-BLUE CORNICE WITH ITS DECORATIONS OF SWANS
AND LYRES, BIRDS FLIT AMONG THE FLOWER GARLANDS.

PAGES 62 AND 63 *A Meissen porcelain service,
and a view of the great lobby, with its gray marble
fountain and antique bust on an unusually tall plinth.*
LEFT, ABOVE, FACING PAGE, AND PAGES 66–67 *The large drawing
room, hung with gray-blue silk damask. The Empire
furniture and the gray and gold ceiling exalting the
sciences, arts, and the military arts lend this room a more
severe and masculine tone than the music room or library,
which reflect Constance's personality.*

RIGHT *Detail of the painted paneling in the dining room.*
FACING PAGE *The moat at the château de Champchevrier, which has been home to the same family since the early eighteenth century.*
PAGES 70–71 *The entrance gates open on to parkland and forest teeming with game, where Louis XI and Louis XIII used to hunt.*

COUNTRY LIFE
AT CHAMPCHEVRIER

FACING PAGE *The pale rays of the October sun light up the music room, decorated with elegant Regency furniture and a set of eighteenth-century tapestries depicting leafy pastoral scenes. Both the furniture and the tapestries are mentioned in an inventory of the château drawn up in 1728 and preserved in the family archives.*

A grand dinner is organized at Champchevrier tonight. We are greeted on the perron stair by Pierre and Béatrice Bizard. Everything is ready. The long table with its damask cloth is decorated with the last roses of autumn and foliage in rich golden shades. I am early, so Béatrice and I wander from one salon to the next; as she tells me the history of the house she throws its doors wide open, right up to the lofty attic rooms.

Lying at the heart of a forested estate in the Loire valley, Champchevrier has been home to the same family since the early eighteenth century. In the sixteenth century, an elegant Renaissance house—whose mullioned windows we still see today—was built on the foundations of a medieval fortress. A century later, a château in the classical style was added to the Renaissance dwelling, with a balustraded terrace looking out over a moat and parkland. In 1728, the estate was bought by Jean-Baptiste de la Rue du Can, who became, by letters patent of Louis XV, Baron de Champchevrier. The present occupants are his direct descendants.

A château such as Champchevrier was traditionally destined to receive guests of rank. These included most particularly the king, whose pleasure it was to hunt in the game-rich forests of an estate where hunting remains to this day firmly anchored at the center of life. Louis XIII was the first sovereign to sleep in the "royal bedchamber," and this must surely be the only château where a king has slept on a bed of straw. According to the archives of Louis XIII's personal physician, "the king arrived at half past six, admired the lake for a while, went to dine and, unable to sleep upon a satin mattress, sent for fresh straw.... On this he lay in his chemise and slept until a quarter past three. Having risen, dressed, and eaten ... he took his harquebus and went down to the farmyard to shoot pigeons." He was just eighteen at the time.

Today the room in which he slept is furnished with a canopy bed and chairs dating from the reign of Louis XVI, covered with a lovely raspberry-colored silk that has its own unexpected story. In 1787–88, according to the archives, the Baronne de Champchevrier and her two daughters decided to cultivate mulberry trees and raise silkworms. They sent their triumphant harvest of 580 silk cocoons to a silk factory in Tours, then the capital of the French silk-weaving industry. Thus it was that they were able to upholster the bed and all the chairs in this room in their own exquisite silk.

In the dining room—also known as the "portrait room"—the floor is of Italian marble, and the Louis XV paneling is decorated with exotic animals, monkeys, parrots, and baskets of fruit and flowers in sepia tones against a background of palest yellow. Behind a little door concealed in the paneling is an antique but still functioning dumb waiter. At the far end of the room, which is now laid out for dinner, stands a great ceramic stove dating from 1780, its flue in the form of a ship's cannon with decorations of dolphins and cannonballs attached by chains. Manufactured by the royal stove-maker—and originally commissioned by the king for the Château de Richelieu—this unique piece lends the dining room a slightly surreal air.

In the two large salons, the fine Regency furniture is surrounded by an outstanding ensemble of seventeenth- and eighteenth-century tapestries, including notably the *Loves of the Gods* and *Voyage of Ulysses* sets, after cartoons by Simon Vouet.

Drawn irresistibly upward—as ever—to the attic rooms, which always bear the stamp of time and of succeeding generations in such a magical way, I find myself high up above the moat, amid a treasure store of memories —a delight to anyone who like me is fascinated by the vestiges of daily life that they contain, the traces of those who lived here in times gone by. Branching off a long passageway running the length of the building are innumerable small

BELOW AND FACING PAGE *Displayed in the tapestry room are two magnificent eighteenth-century sets: the* Loves of the Gods *and* Voyage of Ulysses, *woven at the royal factory at Amiens after cartoons by Simon Vouet, court painter to Louis XIII. The Regency settee, covered with a tapestry after Bérain depicting a group of musicians, adds a vivid splash of color.*

FACING PAGE AND BELOW *In the royal bedchamber, where Louis XIII would sleep after a long day's hunting, the canopy bed and seats are covered with a sumptuous silk made by the château's own silkworms. In 1787, the Baronne de Champchevrier and her two daughters started to breed silkworms as a pastime. That same year they harvested 580 silk cocoons and had this raspberry-colored silk woven at Tours.*

rooms. Wandering through them, I open presses and cupboards, trunks and chests to discover glorious wallpapers and fabrics from the eighteenth and nineteenth centuries, a cornucopia of antique curtains and embroidered white lawns, tassels and fringes, silks, and petit-point tapestries. More trunks and cupboards—all redolent of that evocative fragrance of times past—reveal boxes of wing collars, starched shirt fronts, laces and liveries from every period and—most precious of all—spectacular Louis XVI silk waistcoats and crimson frock coats embroidered in gold. In the linen room, with its poetic simplicity, are neatly folded piles of sheets and towels embroidered with Béatrice's family monogram, tied with pretty pink ribbons.

Béatrice was just twenty-five when she married Pierre Bizard and arrived at Champchevrier. At that time her mother-in-law ran the house like a well-oiled machine, and managed the estate with her son. Gradually, with great tact and delicacy, Béatrice came to know and understand the great house that she has made into a welcoming home for her children and their many cousins. The year 1995 marked a milestone in the history of Champchevrier, when Pierre and Béatrice decided to open the château to the public for three months in the summer; while keeping part of the house for themselves, they cheerfully threw themselves into preparations for welcoming their visitors, and for their new "*vie de château.*"

FACING PAGE *The Baronne de Champchevrier in a white satin dress, painted by Dubufe.*
RIGHT *Laurence, daughter of Pierre and Béatrice, on her wedding day. The marriage was celebrated in the little family chapel (above), which in summer is surrounded by fields of cosmos.*

PAGES 80 AND 81 *The château library.*
BELOW AND FACING PAGE *In the former bedchamber of the Duc de Roquelaure, now a guest room, the four-poster bed in its alcove is covered with a bedspread in Spanish yellow silk with elaborate ivory and pale blue satin appliqué work.*

AS SHE ENTERED, EMMA FELT AS THOUGH SHE WERE ENFOLDED BY THE WARM AIR, IN WHICH THE SCENT OF FLOWERS MINGLED WITH THAT OF FINE LINEN, WITH THE AROMA OF COOKED MEATS AND THE PUNGENCY OF TRUFFLES. THE FLAMES OF THE CANDLES IN THE CANDELABRA CAST LONG REFLECTIONS ON THE SILVER CLOCHES.

GUSTAVE FLAUBERT, *Madame Bovary*

FACING PAGE AND RIGHT *In the large dining room, set for dinner with an antique damask cloth, the paneling is decorated with charming sepia motifs of birds, flowers, and fruit. The walls are hung with family portraits, which watch over the grand dinners traditionally given after the hunt.*
PAGES 86–87 *A little door in the ivory-painted paneling reveals a dumb waiter, still in use today.*

ABOVE AND RIGHT *The dumb waiter (above) and ceramic stove (right) in the dining room. The stove was originally commissioned by the king for the Château de Richelieu, and was bought by the Baron de Champchevrier when the château was demolished in the nineteenth century. Made in around 1780 in the workshops of the Kropper brothers, stove-makers to the king, it is a unique piece, with its flue in the form of a ship's cannon, decorated with dolphins, cannonballs, and chains.*
FACING PAGE *A charming English nineteenth-century plate-warmer. Still in use today, it ensures nice warm plates for guests on winter evenings.*

AND HE WAS SEIZED BY A MORE UNAFFECTED CURIOSITY FOR THE COUNTLESS LITTLE ROOMS THAT—QUITE HEEDLESS OF ANY NOTIONS OF SYMMETRY—TUMBLED ALL AROUND IN ASTONISHMENT, FLEEING IN DISARRAY DOWN TO THE GARDENS. MARCEL PROUST, *The Guermantes Way*

LEFT AND FACING PAGE *Like all grand family houses, the château has a maze of bedrooms through which it is a delight to wander, including the royal bedchamber, the duke's bedchamber, the guest rooms, and numerous simpler bedrooms reserved for the grandchildren and their cousins. What could be more fun than to while away an afternoon poking into cupboards, leafing through old albums, and admiring vintage toys and games?* ABOVE *On the first-floor landing, a painted ceramic stove.*

FINE DAYS ALREADY—LUMINOUS AZURE SKIES AND DUST; WALLS AFLAME AND LENGTHENING DUSK. GÉRARD DE NERVAL, *Avril*

FACING PAGE, BELOW, AND RIGHT *With its restful atmosphere, its scent of freshly laundered linen, and its neatly folded piles of embroidered sheets and napkins, perfectly arranged on shelves and the big ironing table, the laundry room invites you to linger. In a little medicine cabinet are preserved a few antique phials and remedies. One of them, bearing a label inscribed "Droguerie de la pharmacie de l'Hôtel-Dieu de Lyon à Madame la Baronne de Champchevrier, au château de Champchevrier, station de Cléré, Indre-et-Loire," (Drugstore of the Hôtel-Dieu pharmacy in Lyon to the Baronne de Champchevrier, at the château de Champchevrier, Cléré station, Indre-et-Loire) is a reminder of the days when medicines used to be dispatched by train. Their contents remain mysterious, but their faded labels advertise their properties as a panacea for a wide range of maladies.*

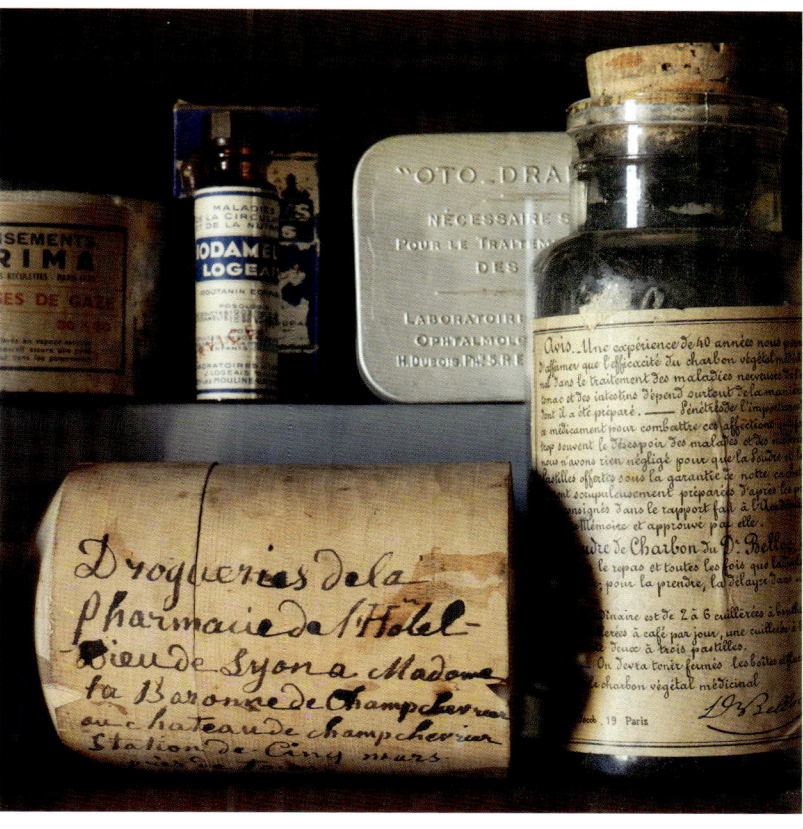

COUNTRY LIFE AT CHAMPCHEVRIER

ONLY RELICS AND VESTIGES CAN SET US DREAMING. RENÉ CHAR, *La Parole en Archipel*

ABOVE AND FACING PAGE *Nothing could be more delightful than exploring the attic rooms and discovering their hidden treasures. Cupboards lining the corridors, boxes, leather trunks, and wicker baskets are filled with marvels: fabrics, wallpapers, tassels, fringes, wing collars, starched fronts, and splendid crimson frock coats embroidered in gold.*
PAGES 96 AND 97 *Eighteenth- and nineteenth-century floral wallpapers, lace curtains, and a Louis XVI silk embroidered waistcoat.*

PRIVATE HOUSES OF FRANCE: LIVING WITH HISTORY

COUNTRY LIFE AT CHAMPCHEVRIER 97

LEFT AND FACING PAGE *Daybreak at Champchevrier. Mist clings to the forest and frost spangles the sweeping lawns as preparations for the hunt get underway. We are to spend the day with the oldest hunt in France, established in 1804, whose master of hounds was for many years Jacques Bizard, a legend in the hunting world.*

A DAY AT THE HUNT
AT CHAMPCHEVRIER

FACING PAGE *The tricolor hounds, of Anglo-French pedigree, are impatient to be off. The Champchevrier kennels today house some ninety hounds.*

Here I am, back at Champchevrier on a misty autumn morning, to spend the day with the oldest hunt in France, on the game-rich lands where Louis XI and Louis XIII loved to hunt. Hunting with hounds is a tradition that is still very much alive in this magnificent wooded landscape, with a history stretching back over more than two centuries. It was in 1804 that the Champchevrier hunt was established, and in 1825 that the Prince de Condé granted to the Baron de Champchevrier the fawn livery with its claret-colored collars and cuffs. The hunt's original mission was to hunt wolves, large numbers of which were still to be found here in the early nineteenth century. When the wolves disappeared, deer and then stags moved into the forests, causing damage to the trees.

The master of the Champchevrier hounds for many years was Jacques Bizard, who has now passed the baton on to his nephew Christophe. Every hunt has its own identity, defined by its livery, its colors, and its hunting horn call. The master of hounds is in charge of the hunt and takes all decisions related to it.

A day with the hounds starts early. Around seven-thirty, the *valets de limier* go out into the forest with dogs that are accustomed to this job, each of them crisscrossing a precisely defined section of forest to track any animal movements. Two hours later they report back to the master of the hounds, who will decide where the hunt should go.

At ten o'clock a loud voice shouts, "*A cheval!*", and everyone mounts. The master of hounds leads off, followed by the whip; surrounding the whip are the hounds, which trot off to the chosen spot. The members of the hunt spread out, then the whip raises his cap and sends the hounds off after the scent. The dogs run past him, baying as they bound off eagerly into the undergrowth.

The riders wait anxiously for a sign. The horses paw the ground impatiently. Then a stag is started by the hounds, and everything begins to move very quickly. For five or six hours, through a forest filled with flaming colors in autumn and covered with a thick blanket of snow or hoar frost in winter, horses and hounds work together.

Stags are clever and fast, and they use a lot of imagination in throwing the hounds off the scent. But the hounds are not easily taken in. Those with the most sensitive noses know their quarry and are not to be distracted. Used to living in a pack and trained up to it, they answer to their names and obey verbal commands, with the younger ones following the lead of their older peers. As in every group, there is sometimes an outsider, an individualist. Great care must be taken not to break his spirit, as he may be the only one to find the scent.

According to Hervé d'Andigné, who interviewed many masters of hounds for his remarkable book on the hunt, "hunting is the science of dogs." If hunting takes place on horseback, it is first and foremost the art of hunting with hounds. It all comes down to the breed, the pedigree, and the dog's behavior and qualities: a booming voice, sturdy endurance, and sensitive nose being the most sought-after attributes. The skill lies in selecting the ones that will make good scent hounds.

Jacques Bizard was an exceptional master of hounds, with a rare understanding both of the forest and of his dogs. The relationship between the master of hounds and his pack is both close and intense, based on a mutual trust which at its finest can produce a curious symbiosis between man and dog. "First and foremost, I used to let my dogs do the hunting, I watched carefully to see how things unfolded, but I left them to it, while at the same time taking care to make sure the pack stayed together. In my life," he goes on, "I have had two exceptional dogs, Javelot and Pénélope. Javelot could bring down a stag on his own. He could run like the wind and was exceptionally intelligent. I lost count of the times when I'd arrive at a lake and wonder

LEFT AND FACING PAGE *Leafing through the hunt's visitors' book and albums, I was surprised to find a photograph taken in the early years of the twentieth century (bottom, left) of my grandmother, Yvonne, Marquise de Nicolay. She wears a long hunting outfit and feathered hat, while the men (top, right) wear long wolfskin coats.*

TRUE HUNTSMEN, LIKE TRUE LOVERS, NEVER SPEAK OF THE OBJECT OF THEIR PASSION. THEY ARE CONTENT TO WORSHIP IT IN THE SILENCE OF THEIR HEARTS. MARQUIS DE FOUDRAS, *Les Gentilshommes Chasseurs*

BELOW *Before setting off on a long day's hunting, Christophe Bizard, who has succeeded his uncle as master of the hounds, entertains guests with a hearty breakfast in the château's vaulted cellars.*
FACING PAGE *Final preparations for the hunt are made in the trophy room.*

104 PRIVATE HOUSES OF FRANCE: LIVING WITH HISTORY

which way to go. Should I head left or right? If Javelot went the opposite way from me he was always right, every time. Pénélope was outstanding too. You could rely on her utterly when it came to following the scent. One day we were following a young stag when we lost the scent and couldn't find it again. We tried everything, but to no avail. On the point of giving up, I doubled back with the hounds to the place where they'd stopped. Then, three hundred meters away, I heard Pénélope baying. Immediately I sounded the '*relance à vue.*' Everyone stared at me, stunned, not understanding how I could give this call without having seen anything. But I knew my dog, and I knew that she'd found her quarry. Twenty minutes later we went in for the kill."

For aficionados, hunting is a true passion, with its own strictly observed ways of doing things and centuries of tradition. The forest, the dogs, the horses, the icy mornings and dazzling landscapes, the return home at dusk and the endless discussions around the fire: the Champchevrier hunt is a day of intense emotion and unforgettable memories.

PAGES 106–7 *The park at break of day.*
ABOVE AND FACING PAGE *In the stables, the horses are also eager to start. Today there are some thirty horses at Champchevrier.*

"IN HUNTING IT IS THE HOUNDS THAT HUNT AND THE HUMANS WHO HELP, NOT THE OTHER WAY ROUND. A HUNTSMAN SHOULD ALWAYS LISTEN TO HIS HOUNDS." JACQUES BIZARD

FACING PAGE AND ABOVE *After visiting the kennels, Béatrice (above, left) greets members of the hunt and guests. In 1825, the Prince de Condé granted the Baron de Champchevrier the privilege of wearing his colors, fawn with claret collars and cuffs.*

"I STARTED OFF WITH TWENTY-THREE HOUNDS. THE NIGHT BEFORE THE HUNT, I WOULD GO OUT TO THE KENNELS AND FEED THEM MYSELF, AND I WOULD DRAW UP A LIST OF THOSE THAT WOULD GO OUT WITH THE NEXT DAY'S HUNT." JACQUES BIZARD

ABOVE, RIGHT, FACING PAGE, AND PAGES 114–15 *The whip, surrounded by the pack, prepares to give the signal for the hunt to start, while the hunt members spread out. Then the hounds are off into the undergrowth, baying as they go, and the horses follow. The hunt is off.*

WHO CAN DESCRIBE THE FEELING AS YOU ENTER THESE FORESTS THAT ARE AS ANCIENT AS THE WORLD, THAT ALONE CAN CONVEY AN IDEA OF CREATION, OF THE WORLD AS GOD MADE IT?

FRANÇOIS-RENÉ DE CHATEAUBRIAND, *Travels in America and Italy*

FACING PAGE, ABOVE, AND RIGHT *The hunt may last for anything up to six hours. In the forest, time seems to hang on the baying of the hounds, the rustling of the leaves beneath the horses' hooves, and glimpses of the quarry.*
PAGES 118–19 *After a long day in the woods, the weary hounds are gathered together on the main lawn.*

"IN THE EVENING I WOULD GO BACK OVER THE HUNT, STAGE BY STAGE, CARRYING ON LATE INTO THE NIGHT IF NEED BE." JACQUES BIZARD

RIGHT AND FACING PAGE *The hunt returns to Champchevrier, where members of the hunt and guests mull over the day. Pierre, our host (right) greets and congratulates everyone individually.*
BELOW, LEFT *The fanfare. A long-established tradition at Champchevrier, hunting is a passion for those who take part in it.*
BELOW, RIGHT *Jacques Bizard on horseback.*
PAGES 122–23 *The evening sun casts its rays through the trees of the forest.*

LEFT AND FACING PAGE *The Château de Condé, in the Picardy region, had the privilege of welcoming the most cultivated spirits of its time. It stands as a beguiling witness to the effervescent spirit of eighteenth-century France and the bucolic charms of Watteau's fêtes galantes.* ABOVE *Portrait of Louis I of Bourbon, first Prince de Condé, who inherited the estate in 1556.*

DISCOVERIES
AT THE CHÂTEAU DE CONDÉ

FACING PAGE *You enter the château through double doors under a semicircular fanlight in the east wing, beneath an arcade. Waiting to greet us at the foot of the main staircase inside are Isabelle de Rochefort and her son Aymeri.*

At the end of a long straight avenue in the Picardy region lies the ancient village of Condé-en-Brie. Here, the Château de Condé, behind a sober classical façade, has a series of surprises in store. Who would guess that once inside they would find themselves in a world of *fêtes galantes* and bucolic flights of fancy, of the wonderfully theatrical, light-hearted spirit of French society in the early eighteenth century? In the great music room decorated by the celebrated Italian-born architect and decorative painter Giovanni Niccolò Servandoni, it takes little effort of the imagination to conjure up the spirited games and brilliant conversations, the parties and balls that these walls have witnessed. Every detail of these elegant surroundings seems to have become imbued with the spirit of the many eminent artists who have stayed here.

The Renaissance château was a stonghold of Louis I of Bourbon, Prince de Condé and leader of the Protestant armies during the first three Wars of Religion, until he met his death at the Battle of Jarnac in 1569. Subsequently it passed to his granddaughter Marie de Savoie-Carignan, who divided her time between the Palazzo Reale in Turin, the Hôtel de Soissons in Paris, and the Château de Condé. It was in 1719 that the Marquis de La Faye bought the estate, which he knew well, having been a guest there on several occasions. An influential figure under the Regency, the marquis was a member of a set of aristocratic patrons and connoisseurs who were great aficionados of travel, culture, and the arts.

In his youth, Jean-François de La Faye had served in the king's musketeers. Having been singled out by Louis XIV for his wit and brilliance, he became a courtier, diplomat, and ambassador to most of the courts of Europe, where he was entrusted with delicate missions including the search for a wife for the young Louis XV. In parallel with his diplomatic activities he was also an accomplished man of affairs and shareholder in the French East India Company, who also owned lands in Louisiana.

His private mansion in Paris contained over two hundred paintings and a vast library, as well as collections of porcelain, bronzes, terra-cotta ware, and marquetry furniture by André-Charles Boulle. A major patron of the arts, he had a particular fondness for the paintings of Watteau and Lancret. His collections of books and objets d'art were among the most important of his day, and at a time before the existence of public museums and galleries—the Musée du Luxembourg was to open in 1750, followed by the Louvre in 1793—he opened his *hôtel particulier* to a select public.

In the latter years of Louis XIV's reign, it was fashionable to entertain in the more relaxed, pastoral atmosphere of the country; accordingly, the Marquis de La Faye decided to make Condé his country house. Highly respected already as a connoisseur and patron of the arts, he was to use this as an opportunity to treat a large number of artists to his generous patronage. After commissioning Nicolas Lancret to paint a set of canvases on the theme of the seasons, he was so delighted with the first two paintings that he doubled the agreed fee on the spot. To the celebrated animal painter Jean-Baptiste Oudry, meanwhile, he granted an annuity of two hundred livres and a contract of lavish generosity. Summoned to the château in 1721, Oudry worked for the marquis until 1725, painting notably four enormous canvases on the theme of hunting and fishing, and subtle paneling paintings in shades of almond green for the dining room, now a drawing room.

In the music room, also called the billiards room, Servandoni deployed his full talents as a trompe l'oeil artist, taking his inspiration from the Carracci brothers' work at the Palazzo Farnese in Rome. On immense canvases hung on the walls, he painted virtuoso architectural scenes of columns and pilasters, statues and Romanesque arches in tones of pink and apricot, interspersed with accomplished scenes in grisaille. Above the marble fireplace

he depicted *The Rape of Proserpina by Pluto*, and on the east wall *Apollo and the Nymphs*.

Jean-François de La Faye's "most dear friend" and muse was Jeanne de Luynes, Comtesse de Verrue, who inspired Alexandre Dumas's novel *La Dame de Volupté*. Clever, influential, and passionate about art, she too was a great patron of the artists of her time and a champion of French aesthetics and refinement in taste. Having survived the Revolution unscathed, the estate passed in 1814 to the Sade family.

Nearly two hundred years later, in 1983, Alain and Isabelle Pasté de Rochefort became the new owners of Condé. With support from the Monuments Historiques, they embarked on a lengthy restoration campaign—a major undertaking that was to be rewarded with some handsome discoveries. In the drawing room painted by Oudry, for example, they were astonished to find, hidden behind the overmantel mirror, a painting of a scene from a short story by Jean de La Fontaine, *La Fiancée du Roi de Garbe*. It was signed with the letter "W". Could this be a Watteau? The question remains open.

Another surprise lay in store in the room known as the "musician's bedchamber": behind layer upon layer of wallpaper and several thicknesses of newspapers dating from the period of the Revolution—used as insulation— there suddenly appeared a feature that had been totally forgotten: a little secret door topped with a painting by Lancret. And, more recently, other works have been discovered.

Now that Isabelle has sadly lost her husband, it is with her son Aymeri that she continues to restore life and soul to this great house, so perpetuating the genius loci, the charmingly lighthearted spirit of Watteau's *fêtes galantes*.

LEFT *Detail of one of the many decorative paintings on the antechamber walls, depicting landscapes in the region of Condé-en-Brie.*
FACING PAGE *The château's oldest staircase.*

THE SKY SO PALE AND THE TREES SO SPINDLY
SEEM TO SMILE ON THE LIGHT GOWNS
WE WEAR, FLOATING, FILMY, WITH AN AIR
OF LANGUID FLUTTERING IN THE BREEZE.

PAUL VERLAINE, *À la Promenade*

FACING PAGE *The chimney breast in the musician's bedchamber is decorated with a delightful painted scene of a couple dancing to flute music, a reprise of the theme of the painting of Autumn, commissioned from Lancret by the Marquis de La Faye.*
BELOW *A trompe l'oeil scene of a painter and a musician leaning on a balustrade at the end of a passage epitomizes the light-hearted spirit that enlivens all the château's rooms.*

ART IS SOMETHING THAT LIES IN THE SLENDER MARGIN BETWEEN THE REAL AND THE UNREAL. CHIKAMATSU MONZAEMON

PAGES 132–33, ABOVE, RIGHT, AND FACING PAGE *The large salon or music room—formerly given over entirely to dance, theater, and music—is decorated with remarkable trompe l'oeil paintings by Servandoni, executed in 1724 and inspired by the work of the Carracci brothers at the Palazzo Farnese. Columns and statues, pilasters and grisailles all create an extraordinary illusion of reality in this trompe l'oeil architecture. On the chimney breast, the* Rape of Proserpina *adds a theatrical ambience. A niche holds a graceful depiction of* Apollo and the Nymphs *behind a faux balustrade.*

FROM ROOM TO ROOM I BREATHED IN
THAT AROMA OF OLD LIBRARIES, FILLING
THE AIR LIKE INCENSE, THAT BEATS EVERY
OTHER PERFUME IN THE WORLD.
ANTOINE DE SAINT-EXUPÉRY, *Wind, Sand and Stars*

FACING PAGE AND BELOW *Paneling in the library and the enfilade of salons.*
PAGE 138 *This anteroom was put at the disposal of Watteau and his pupils—including Pater and Lancret—and served as their studio. The walls are hung with landscapes of the local area.*
PAGE 139 The Pedlar *(detail).*

HE RECEIVED TWO GIFTS FROM THE GODS, THE MOST DELIGHTFUL THAT THEY COULD OFFER: ONE WAS A TALENT TO PLEASE, THE OTHER THE GIFT OF BEING HAPPY. VOLTAIRE, on the Marquis de La Faye

FACING PAGE, ABOVE, AND PAGES 142–43 *The dining room is now a salon, decorated with four very large canvases commissioned by the Marquis de La Faye from Jean-Baptiste Oudry, official painter of hunting scenes to Louis XV, which depict the return from the hunt and the return from a fishing expedition. Oudry also carried out the decorative paintings on the paneling, charming camaïeux in shades of green, gray, and gold depicting trompe l'oeil garlands of oak leaves and hunting motifs.*

BELOW *Detail of one of Oudry's paintings for the dining room,* Swan Turning toward a Still Life of Fish and Fowl.
FACING PAGE *Set into the almond-green paneling is another Oudry painting on a hunting theme,* Dead Wolf, *featuring a fruit-laden buffet at its center.*

144   PRIVATE HOUSES OF FRANCE: LIVING WITH HISTORY

SILENCE IS THE SOUL OF THINGS THAT WISH TO KEEP A SECRET.
IT VANISHES AT THE BREAK OF DAY, TO RETURN IN THE ROSY LIGHT
OF SUNSET. MAURICE ROLLINAT, *Le Silence*

FACING PAGE *Isabelle's small salon in one of the turrets.*
ABOVE *The Richelieu bedchamber, named after
the cardinal who stayed at Condé when he came
to hold talks with the young Mazarin.
The four-poster bed is dressed with crimson silk.*
RIGHT *"Jeune accouchée" (young mother) bedspread
in embroidered fine lawn.*

LEFT AND ABOVE *Princesse G.'s grandmother on horseback, and a rock crystal flask with a lapis lazuli stopper set with pearls and brilliant-cut diamonds.*
FACING PAGE *Red is omnipresent in the princess's apartment near the Champs-Élysées, striking a cheerful note that chimes with her eternal optimism. In the salon, a very fine divan à la turque stands in front of a dazzling Brussels tapestry depicting the story of the Golden Fleece.*

CHILDHOOD MEMORIES
OF PRINCESSE G.

FACING PAGE *A "little note with a bouquet of flowers" sent to Princesse G. by the painter, interior designer, and costume designer Christian Bérard in 1945.*

Today, my friend Princesse G. and I are dipping into almost a century of memories. They begin on avenue Montaigne, where the princess spent her childhood with her parents, sisters, and paternal grandparents, in a Paris that was very different from the city we know today. Her early years were marked by World War II. The Germans occupied the family's country estate, amid aerial bombardments on all sides. After her beloved father was killed at Calais in May 1940 she found herself alone. She decided to stay on in order to look after the house and to help the local villagers by allowing them to use the cellars as a shelter.

When the war was over she went back to Paris, where she found friends among a celebrated set of aesthetes and patrons of art, all of them older than she was, who were to have a lasting influence on the development of twentieth-century taste: brilliant, sophisticated, and hugely talented artists such as Charles and Marie-Laure de Noailles, Carlos de Beistegui, Emilio Terry, Christian Bérard, and Édouard and Denise Bourdet. This unforgettable era was a time of glittering balls and parties for the princess, which she followed up with major voyages of discovery in Asia and America.

Having looked after a large French country estate for so many years, Princesse G. now chooses to spend most of her time in Paris. Today I find her in her Faubourg-Saint-Germain apartment, surrounded by objets d'art, drawings, family paintings, and personal mementos. She greets me in her salon lined with red velvet, and I listen with delight as this grand old lady, sharp as a pin, shares her memories of childhood.

She explains that her father, an officer in the navy, always longed for a son, and finding himself instead with three daughters declared that they were all foolish and would never marry! But the girls adored him anyway and paid no attention: life was good, they were pretty and charming, and Paris was at their feet.

Going back even further, to the time when she lived in her grandparents' house on avenue Montaigne, she remembers with a smile: "The ground floor was a place of delights for us. From the great gloomy anteroom you went into light, cheerful rooms looking out over avenue Montaigne. On the other side of the street, the horse dealer Barlett would put his mounts through their paces. My grandfather was a great connoisseur of art, who over the years collected numerous objets d'art and precious ornaments: looking back on it all now, I can see that everything in that great house was in harmony and in the most beautiful taste.

"In pride of place in the main drawing room was a full-length portrait of the Duchesse de Montmorency surrounded by her children. The pretty little girl holding a posy of flowers beside the young Prince de Tancarville was the future Duchesse de Rohan, my father's great-grandmother. I have taken great care to preserve this painting, and it now hangs over the fireplace.

"The grandmother's small drawing room was intimate and comfortable, and we knew every nook and cranny of it—her well-ordered bureau, her bookcase, her deep bergère chairs, and her innumerable paintings and family photographs. In a mahogany armoire were the remains of the trousseau that Virtudes—my grandmother's first name—had brought with her as a young bride: dozens of pairs of stockings in pastel colors, camisoles trimmed with Valenciennes lace, and curious bloomers split down the middle that we never tired of marveling at.

"All the rooms were filled with a particular scent, a mixture of the perfume of iris from the cupboards and the fragrance of the potpourri oils in the copper perfume-burner in the antechamber.

"For the little girls that we then were, the servants' quarters were even more fascinating, and thanks to our governess Marcella we were allowed free run of them. In the laundry room,

"I HAVE MEMORIES, BUT ABOVE ALL I HAVE PLANS. THERE ARE STILL SO MANY THINGS TO DO AND KNOW." PRINCESSE G.

FACING PAGE *Above the fireplace in the salon hangs a large eighteenth-century portrait of the Duchesse de Montmorency and her children.*
ABOVE, LEFT *Princesse G. at the Hôtel Beistegui at 3, rue de Constantine, Paris, beside Emilio Terry's famous door veneered in ebony and mahogany. In the post-war years, the princess was very close to the celebrated circle of Parisian aesthetes and connoisseurs, architects, artists, and designers who included Charles and Marie-Laure de Noailles, Carlos de Beistegui, and Emilio Terry.*
ABOVE, RIGHT *Part of the princess's collection of precious objects by Fabergé.*

there would be flat irons heating around the hexagonal wood stove. As she ironed the pin-tucks and frills on my grandmother's nightgowns, Mrs Eden, the widow of the English coachman, used to tell us charming stories about the Victorian house where she used to live, and we were riveted by her tales of the little details and events of English life, all related with a strong Cockney accent. Behind her irreproachably respectable exterior, Mrs Eden was a victim of the demon drink: one day we found her flat out on the bathroom floor, rather the worse for wear for having drunk a bottle of eau de cologne!

"The butler was a rather dour character, who had once—in happier circumstances, doubtless—made the young lady's maid pregnant. My mother quickly spotted the maid's thickening waistline and told my grandmother, who refused to believe it, accusing her daughter-in-law of having a suspicious mind. She was extraordinarily good and kind by nature, and she showered us, her granddaughters, with endless love and affection.

"When my mother's firstborn came along she didn't have enough milk to feed this hungry baby (me!), so she put the baby out to a wet nurse, the wife of a miner from Asturias. The workers from this region tended strongly toward Marxism, and the sight of his wife neglecting their own baby in order to 'squander her milk on the daughter of a marquis' can't have done much to dissuade her husband from his determination to abolish the inequalities of society!"

Princesse G.'s childhood memories paint a portrait in miniature of a vanished Paris, and a vivid picture of life in the happy house on avenue Montaigne nearly a century ago. Now nearly ninety, she seems to possess the secret of eternal youth, constantly curious, constantly amusing, with deadpan humor and wide-ranging wit. It is impossible to be bored in her company. With her iron self-discipline, insatiable curiosity, astonishing vitality, and that twinkle in her eye, she finds amusement in everything and is up for anything: life around her is filled with the scent of eternal spring.

LEFT *Arranged on a small table in the salon are an eighteenth-century Neapolitan tortoiseshell and mother-of-pearl box given to the princess's grandmother by the Duchesse de Morny, and a tortoiseshell and gold paper knife and pill box.*
ABOVE *Young Woman with a Ruff,* pen-and-ink *drawing by Watteau.*
FACING PAGE *Portrait of a Woman in a Blue Dress, one of the princess's eighteenth-century ancestors.*

FASHIONS PASS; STYLE NEVER. COCO CHANEL

PAGES 156–57 AND FACING PAGE
The large salon, lined with red velvet, has a warm and welcoming atmosphere.
ABOVE *Sketch by Christian Bérard published in Vogue in 1935.*
RIGHT *The prodigiously talented Christian Bérard with one of his models, photographed by Roger Schall.*

BELOW *Bust of a girl by Carrier-Belleuse, and Princesse G.'s mother wearing a Spanish shawl, by Étienne Adrien Drian, c.1920.*
FACING PAGE *Some of the princess's collection of pieces by Fabergé: a perfume bottle, bell pulls, and a seal.*

160 PRIVATE HOUSES OF FRANCE: LIVING WITH HISTORY

ABOVE *Assouan, a faithful friend.*
FACING PAGE *Hubert de Givenchy welcomes us into his home, the magnificent Hôtel d'Orrouer in the Faubourg-Saint-Germain, built in 1732 by Pierre Boscry. The garden façade is remarkable for its highly unusual "tiara" pediment.*

THE ELEGANCE
OF HUBERT DE GIVENCHY

Hubert de Givenchy, the legendary couturier, is arranging the flowers one evening in October—beautiful white hyacinths—for a dinner that he is giving for a few friends on the first floor of his Paris *hôtel particulier*. The ground floor of this splendid residence—the Hôtel d'Orrouer, built in 1732 by the architect Pierre Boscry for the Comte d'Orrouer, and later occupied by a number of distinguished figures including the Comtesse de Boisgelin, the Duc de Montmorency, the Duc de Bauffremont, and Prince von Metternich—has already featured in another of my books.

Hubert de Givenchy bought this exceptional residence in 1986. In 1993, having decided to move from the first floor to the ground floor, he put some of his furniture and his remarkable collection of artworks up for sale at Christie's, including a silver chandelier designed by William Kent in 1736, antique marbles, Venetian bronzes, and precious marquetry furniture by André-Charles Boulle. But his passion for art and objets d'art proved unstoppable, and he could not resist starting a new collection and redecorating the first floor, which he metamorphosed once again into a "palace of wonders."

As you enter the grand salon, hung with green velvet, it is impossible not to be dazzled by the famous "*goût Givenchy*." If perfect taste, or perfect style, exists, like perfect pitch in music, then this is it, unfolding before our eyes. In all the places that bear the Givenchy stamp—the Château du Jonchet, his country house in the Eure-et-Loire department, and his various other houses—it is impossible not to admire his peerless taste, and his effortless gift for creating witty mixes of different eras and styles, classic and modern, Grand Siècle, and contemporary.

As Hubert de Givenchy talks about various episodes in his life, I begin to understand what a tremendous effect it had on him when, as a very young man working for Schiaparelli, he made his first visit to Misia Sert. Misia—who had been the "Queen of Paris," muse to painters, poets, and musicians—had created a singular harmony of forms, textures, and objects that were wildly eclectic, mixing Boulle marquetry furniture with modern paintings; gold and bronze with tortoiseshell, mother-of-pearl, and crystal; and accumulating collections of Chinese lacquer ware, Coromandel screens, and curiosities. Her husband, the Catalan-born painter and decorative artist José Maria Sert, never let a day go by without buying some objet d'art, drawing, or piece of furniture. Their collection was legendary.

Misia Sert's apartment was the meeting place for the celebrities of the time, a magical world where artists and patrons could mix in complete freedom, including Marie-Laure de Noailles, Marie-Blanche de Polignac, Marie-Louise Bousquet, Bérard, Cocteau, Sauguet, and Poulenc. Hubert de Givenchy was never to forget his first visit, and his *coup de foudre* for the hugely inventive way in which the apartment was decorated, which

FACING PAGE *The large white salon on the first floor, a marvel of elegance, beauty, and serenity, epitomizes the "goût Givenchy." In front of the window, a very fine bureau by the cabinetmaker Joseph.*
RIGHT *Portrait of Hubert de Givenchy by his friend, the photographer Victor Skrebneski.*

FACING PAGE *The large red morocco-bound volumes laid out on the bureau are part of a set given to the Comte de Montmorin by Louis XVI.* BELOW *One of a pair of seventeenth-century German bronze stags.*

was to have an enduring influence on his taste. When later he moved into rue Fabert and bought Misia's famous "Chariot of Apollo" Boulle armoire, he deliberately hung a Rothko painting opposite it. It was a founding gesture, the beginning of the credo to which he has remained faithful ever since, favoring the combination (rather than the opposition) of ancient and modern.

In all his houses, Hubert de Givenchy sets up a sort of interrupted dialogue between very diverse artists: seventeenth-century Italian bronzes rub shoulders with furniture by Diego Giacometti and a large Picasso drawing; periods and styles mix together quite naturally, as if they were always meant to. Reigning over all is a skillful balance, a harmony, and a sense of peace.

In the salon overlooking the garden of white roses, sunlight picks out the magnificent white and gold boiseries by the celebrated sculptor and decorative artist Nicolas Pineau. The light is reflected in two immense mirrors, facing each other. A pair of magnificent marble and gilt bronze vases stands before the french windows, which are framed by curtains in ivory faille. On the tables are rare and delicate objects, all of them chosen with care.

As night falls the candles are lit, patiently, one by one, in the salon opening on to the inner courtyard. The walls are hung with an emerald green velvet that sets off perfectly the remarkable seventeenth-century embroidered curtains from the residence of Baron Élie de Rothschild on rue Masseran.

Elegance and discretion, restraint and harmony: the residence of Hubert de Givenchy is the image of his very special brand of chic. As always in his world of elegance, whether in the impeccable cut of an evening gown, the sophisticated fragrance of a perfume, or the choice and arrangement of a group of remarkable objects, this perfect taste betrays a private obsession: a tireless quest for beauty.

ABOVE *Hubert de Givenchy on a trip to Japan with his muse and friend Audrey Hepburn. From his first introduction to her on the set of* Sabrina, *Givenchy was Hepburn's couturier of choice; she in turn was the embodiment of his special brand of chic.*
RIGHT *The rue de Rivoli apartment of José Maria and Misia Sert. It was here that Givenchy, then a young assistant to Schiaparelli, experienced the aesthetic coup de foudre that was to have such an enduring influence on his taste.*
FACING PAGE *On the mantelpiece, a pair of Chinese "black mirror" vases; in the fireplace, a pair of gilt bronze firedogs from the famous collection of the Duchesse de Mazarin.*

EVERY CHERISHED OBJECT IS THE CENTRAL POINT OF A PARADISE. NOVALIS

LEFT *A chair covered in a magnificent Genoa velvet fabric.*
ABOVE AND FACING PAGE *A silver-gilt goblet; on the table, is a characteristically Givenchy collection of objets d'art: a Chinese lacquer potpourri vase, a little dog in gilt bronze, porcelain, rock crystal, and a posy of fresh flowers.*

"I SEEK HARMONY ABOVE ALL THINGS." HUBERT DE GIVENCHY

FACING PAGE AND LEFT *A remarkable pair of Louis XV marble and gilt bronze vases, embellished with satyr masks and entwined snakes, flanks the central tall window overlooking the garden.*
ABOVE *A falcon adorns the lid of a Japanese taka-maki-e lacquer box.*
PAGES 174-75 *The grand salon, with its white and gold boiseries by the celebrated decorative sculptor Nicolas Pineau, and its majestic rock crystal and gilt bronze chandelier.*

WHERE OTHERS HAVE PERFECT PITCH,
HUBERT DE GIVENCHY HAS A PERFECT EYE.

BELOW *A still life of silver-gilt precious objets.*
FACING PAGE *Behind the small Louis XV bureau and the Étienne Meunier armchair in petit point, a magnificent gilt bronze Regency fire screen from the Hôtel de Castries.*

LEFT AND ABOVE *A period bathroom looks out over the garden, which is filled with "Iceberg" roses.*
FACING PAGE *The guest room, as big as a salon, boasts an extremely rare double cornice by Nicolas Pineau, who worked with Pierre Boscry on the decorations of the Hôtel d'Orrouer.*
PAGES 180 AND 181 *The green salon overlooking the inner courtyard has sumptuous seventeenth-century silk curtains embroidered with a floral design in colored silks and gold and silver thread, which came from the Hôtel de Masseran, former residence of Baron and Baroness Élie de Rothschild. A small chauffeuse beside the fireplace is covered with the same embroidered silk.*

BELOW AND FACING PAGE *Above the marble fireplace in the green salon is a large gilt bronze Louis XIV mirror. The magnificent gilt bronze firedogs are from the collection of Cardinal de Bernis. The bellows, by André-Charles Boulle, sit on a Louis XIV stool covered in velvet.*

ABOVE AND FACING PAGE *Details of the embroidered curtains and cushions in the green salon. Beside the sofa, a collection of rare objets d'art in silver, silver gilt, and bronze.*

IMAGINATION SEEMS TO BE DISTILLED TO SUBTLETY AND TASTE TO QUINTESSENCE; WITH FANTASY, INGENUITY, AND ABANDON, THE TOUR DE FORCE IS ACCOMPLISHED. ADRIEN FAUCHIER-MAGNAN

LEFT AND ABOVE *Hubert de Givenchy has arranged candles and white hyacinths on the console on the first-floor landing to welcome his guests as they pass by on their way to the green salon, filling the evening with a dream-like ambience.*
FACING PAGE *Above a commode by André-Charles Boulle, a portrait of the financier Étienne-Michel Bouret displaying the royal pavilion of Croix-Fontaine is seen by candlelight, as in the eighteenth century.*
PAGES 188–89 *Flickering candlelight on green velvet creates an atmosphere reminiscent of Visconti's* The Leopard *in the green salon.*

LEFT *Reflections of the pale boiseries of the entrance hall in a crystal ball.*
FACING PAGE *In this pretty eighteenth-century hôtel particulier, the owner has been able to give free rein to her lifelong passion for "le goût français." The library is decorated with a trompe l'oeil painting given to the Duke and Duchess of Windsor by Tony Duquette around 1950, which creates the illusion of more bookshelves. On the low lacquer table, the owner has displayed part of her collection of straw marquetry boxes and a telescope with a red morocco case bearing the French royal coat of arms.*

AN AMERICAN IN PARIS

Susan G. is an American in love with France, who has always had a passion for French taste, and who adores style and fashion in all their subtlest variations. When she came to live in Paris with her husband John some twenty years ago, it was an opportunity to make a dream come true: to set up home in a glorious eighteenth-century Parisian *hôtel particulier*.

She had previously entrusted the decoration of her New York apartment to the great French interior designer Henri Samuel, who had become a friend. When she arrived in Paris she turned to him again, while also asking the architect Alain Raynaud to restore the rooms to their original volumes and classical proportions. Celebrated for his opulent interiors—for Louise de Vilmorin, the Vanderbilts, and the Aga Khan, among others—Henri Samuel was unrivaled in his ability to display a collection to best effect. He had already deployed this talent on the Rothschild collections, for which he created a perfectly judged marriage of eighteenth-century boiseries, old masters, and contemporary works, and of furniture in classical style and modern sculptures. This apartment for Susan was to be his final project, an elegant and luxurious swan song.

Susan greets me in the library on a lovely spring day. A subtle but vivid palette creates an ambience full of charm and character: yellow ocher walls, an almond-green sofa, a pretty collection of straw marquetry boxes on a low red lacquer table. A large trompe l'oeil painting above the sofa complements the bookcases, with skillful echoes of their antique bindings. Arranged on the Regency *bureau plat* are handsome volumes bound in red morocco and a magnificent Louis XV telescope in a morocco case bearing the French royal coat of arms.

Moving on from the library, the pale spring sunlight falls on the Versailles parquet of the large Louis XVI salon, beneath the magnificent crystal and amethyst chandelier. The light glows softly on a collection of paintings in *verre églomisé* in the white and silver tones with which the whole room is washed, making it both luminous and serene. The scroll-armed sofa and armchairs upholstered in pale gray velvet were designed by Henri Samuel after the "*canapés de Monsieur*" in the private apartments at Versailles. On the tables, collections of ivory objets contrast with black porcelain Qing dynasty vases.

As the light begins to fade, we go to the Directoire dining room on the ground floor, opening on to the entrance courtyard. In the evening, candles illumine its paneling painted with allegorical scenes, their light reflected in numerous mirrors and flickering on the Chantilly porcelain dinner service and the Bohemian glasses.

In the blue salon, lovely Louis XVI "wallpaper" curtains, perfectly preserved, display all the astonishing freshness of their original colors. The chairs in front of the window have blue cotton covers with late eighteenth-century appliqué decoration by Mary Delany, famed at the court of George III for her embroideries and exquisite hand-colored "paper-mosaiks [*sic*]."

Susan leads me up to the second floor, where her bedroom, with its flower-patterned canopy bed, walls, and curtains, is like a rose garden, or a bouquet of freshly gathered blooms. The boudoir, in tones of cream and blue-gray, is a haven of tranquility, where she has had the floor painted in a pretty combination of blue and ivory. The fireplace contains a trompe l'oeil painting by Jeffrey Bailey of three large blue-and-white Chinese porcelain vases. A very Proustian *chauffeuse* in blue satin with a removable "hood" invites you to hide away from the hustle and bustle of the city with a good book. Susan tells me that hoods such as these were brought into fashion by Madame de Maintenon, who adopted them as a defense against the icy draughts of Versailles.

Susan and John have now gone back to live in America, taking with them a gentle nostalgia for Paris. But, as Susan says with a smile, quoting Humphrey Bogart's words in the final scene of *Casablanca*, "We'll always have Paris."

PAGES 192 AND 193 *Eighteenth-century straw marquetry boxes and cases, with a detail of the lovely tablecloth in sea-green moiré embroidered with flowers.*
FACING PAGE *The first-floor enfilade. With the help of the great interior designer Henri Samuel and the architect Alain Raynaud, Susan restored these lovely rooms to their original proportions, adding fine Louis XVI boiseries.*

BELOW AND FACING PAGE *A magnificent Italian rock crystal and amethyst chandelier hangs in the light-flooded grand salon. On the walls is a collection of verre églomisé compositions in tones of gold and gray, painted by the German artist Jonas Zeuner around 1800. Beside the sofa and armchairs—designed by Henri Samuel after models in the "apartments of Monsieur" at Versailles—stands an eighteenth-century embroidered screen with motifs of flowers and birds (detail below).*

LEFT AND FACING PAGE *As evening draws in, the candles are lit in the Directoire dining room decorated with lovely neoclassical painted panels. For dinner, Susan has chosen one of her many Chantilly porcelain services and engraved Bohemian crystal glasses.*

OUR REALM SHALL BE A DISCREET BOUDOIR, ALWAYS IMBUED WITH A FRAGRANCE DIVINE, ALLOWING IN, AS MAY BE DIVINED, BUT A TWILIGHT GLOW, SOFT AND WEAK. GERMAIN NOUVEAU, *Sonnet d'Été*

FACING PAGE, RIGHT, AND BELOW *The pretty boudoir is a haven from the hubbub of the city. The trio of large blue-and-white Chinese vases in the fireplace is in fact a trompe l'oeil painting by the artist Jeffrey Bailey. The cushions, painted silk, lace curtains, and painted paneling create delicate harmonies of blues, grays, and whites.*
PAGES 202 AND 203 *Detail of an early nineteenth-century Paris porcelain cachepot decorated with swags and flowers, and a fine china tea service.*

AN AMERICAN IN PARIS 201

A ROOM THAT IS LIKE A REVERIE, A ROOM THAT IS TRULY SPIRITUAL, WHERE THE MOTIONLESS AIR IS LIGHTLY TINGED WITH BLUE AND PINK.

CHARLES BAUDELAIRE, *Little Poems in Prose*

LEFT AND FACING PAGE *The remarkable curtains in the blue salon, made using a Louis XVI wallpaper, lend the room an air of wonderfully dainty freshness. The chair has a cotton cover with late eighteenth-century appliqué embroidery by Mary Delany, celebrated at the court of George III for her "paper-mosaiks [sic]."*

RIGHT AND FACING PAGE *Near Parc Monceau, the family home of art connoisseur Édouard stands in a delightful secret garden, a leafy jungle of ferns, bamboos, and cushions of box and moss. A pair of dogs seems completely at home in this leafy paradise.*

ANCESTRAL TREASURES
IN PARC MONCEAU

A leafy bower near Parc Monceau—one of those secret gardens that are so inimitably Parisian—frames the *hôtel particulier* that I am visiting today. There, I am greeted by Édouard, a fine art connoisseur, who over the years has become a favored consultant to some of the world's greatest collectors. Since childhood he has nurtured a passion for historic furniture, paintings, and objets d'art, and in so doing has followed a time-honored family tradition.

In the late nineteenth century his American great-grandfather, a property magnate in San Francisco, made a trip to Europe. So dazzled was he by Paris and its architecture that he decided to settle there. Then he met a young Frenchwoman, fell in love, and married her. Still consumed by a passion for building, he bought numerous plots in Paris and the surrounding area, where he continued to build apartment blocks and houses. When he died suddenly five years later, his wife continued his work with tremendous energy.

It was she who moved into this handsome residence on the edge of Parc Monceau with her two children—whose marble portrait sculptures now stand beside the large window opening on to the garden. Her daughter—our host's grandmother—inherited her indomitable character, and in her youth loved to go to the major auctions at the Hôtel Drouot, slipping off there in search of new treasures on a virtually daily basis. There are stories of her clambering among rush baskets and scaling packing cases and tottering piles of boxes, undaunted in her search for the next fabulous piece. At this period, Paris was the capital of the world art market, and the Hôtel Drouot, opened in 1852, was the most important art auction house in the world, hosting legendary sales such as the extraordinary collections of the couturier Jacques Doucet in 1912. She was probably there.

Thus she filled her salons with furniture, old paintings, and objets d'art, as well as a magnificent collection of eighteenth-century porcelain. Whirling from one party to the next and one discovery to the next, she lived to the full the opulent, extravagant life of fashionable Belle Époque Paris. "But when she grew old," my host explains, "my grandmother decided to shut up the vast ground floor—reserved, she said, for parties—completely, to cover the furniture with dust sheets, to pack her innumerable treasures away in commodes, armoires, and chests of drawers, and to withdraw to her bedroom to live in peaceful seclusion."

"As children," he goes on, "my cousins and I never tired of exploring this intriguing house in which time seemed to have stood still, a wonderful setting for games and adventures, mysteries and dreams.... In the darkness of its shuttered rooms, we would surreptitiously lift dust sheets and covers, we would find the keys for the great armoires, and we would compare our discoveries. A visit to our grandmother was far more exciting than going to the cinema: it was like going back in time and discovering buried treasure. This house in Parc Monceau played a hugely important part in my childhood, and in influencing my tastes—not to say my future life. I believe I have inherited my grandmother's insatiable curiosity and her love of beauty, and it's a passion that I love to share."

FACING PAGE *Beside the window overlooking the garden stands a large sculpture of two children by Jules-Jacques Labatut. The little girl with such a lively expression is our host's grandmother, who in the early years of the twentieth century would go to the Hôtel Drouot every day in search of new treasures.*
ABOVE *Édouard's American great-grandfather, a property magnate from San Francisco, came to Paris in the late nineteenth century, married, and never left.*

WHAT MUST THE ATTICS BE LIKE, WHEN THE SALON CONTAINED THE RICHES OF AN ATTIC! WHEN YOU GUESSED THAT THE HALF-OPEN DOORS OF THE MOST INSIGNIFICANT CUPBOARD MIGHT DISGORGE BUNDLES OF YELLOWING LETTERS, GREAT-GRANDFATHER'S RECEIPTS, AND MORE KEYS THAN THERE WERE LOCKS IN THE HOUSE. ANTOINE DE SAINT-EXUPÉRY, *Wind, Sand and Stars*

PAGES 210 AND 211 *The yellow salon opening on to the garden is home to a harmonious mixture of Chinese objets d'art and family portraits and mementoes.*
BELOW AND FACING PAGE *Objects and mementoes of times past: a capacious silver wine cooler, porcelain coffee cans, and a charming photograph of Édouard's grandmother.*

FACING PAGE *Édouard's grandmother's blond tortoiseshell and swan's-down fan set with brilliants, made by the house of Duvelleroy.*
BELOW *A pair of rare "fire salamander" ceramic vases ceramic from Gien, a Chinese jade bowl, and Édouard's intrepid grandmother photographed in evening dress with her three children.*

ANCESTRAL TREASURES IN PARC MONCEAU 215

WONDROUS KEYS WITHOUT A USE, KEYS THAT CONFUSED OUR THOUGHTS, MAKING US DREAM OF UNDERGROUND CHAMBERS, BURIED CASKETS, AND LOUIS D'OR. ANTOINE DE SAINT-EXUPÉRY, *Wind, Sand and Stars*

LEFT *Half a dozen champagne flutes from a service from Malmaison, residence of Empress Josephine.*
ABOVE *Portrait of Queen Hortense with her children, including the future Napoleon III.*
FACING PAGE *Behind a handsome silver fruit presentoir, a Jane Eyre–like figure eyes us quizzically from a nineteenth-century painting.*

216 PRIVATE HOUSES OF FRANCE: LIVING WITH HISTORY

LEFT AND FACING PAGE *The lovely Renaissance château of Montrésor, set in the Touraine countryside, reflected in the waters of the River Indrois. In the entrance courtyard stands a striking life-size statue of Mieczyslaw Kamienski, a young Polish officer and cousin of Count Xavier Branicki, ancestor of the present owners of Montrésor, who was killed at the Battle of Magenta.*

ROMANTICISM AND NOSTALGIA
AT MONTRÉSOR

FACING PAGE *A portrait photograph taken in the 1920s of a cousin of Countess Stanislas Rey, one of the present owners of Montrésor, in a silver frame decorated with cupids.*

A pretty village in Touraine, with narrow winding streets leading up to a Renaissance château surrounded by greenery: we are in the heart of the Loire country, and—though we do not yet know it—as we enter the château grounds we are about to be transported into another world, one that is tinged with a gentle air of Slavic melancholy.

Inside the gates, it is impossible not to be struck by a remarkable life-size bronze sculpture of a young man, half-reclining and about to die. Who is he? Later we learn that this statue was raised here in memory of Mieczyslaw Kamienski, a young Polish officer killed at the Battle of Magenta in 1859, after fighting alongside his cousin Count Branicki, ancestor of our hosts. And so we are plunged into the fascinating history of Montrésor.

Ten years earlier, in 1849, Count Xavier Branicki, a wealthy Polish nobleman who had fled his country, settled in France and bought Montrésor. A liberal, a staunch Bonapartist, and an entrepreneur with a passionate interest in modern progress, he had been an opponent of Czar Nicholas II—to the extent of financing the opposition newspaper—and so had been forced into permanent exile. When he arrived at Montrésor, the French minister of the interior had him put under surveillance as part of a secret agenda aimed at expelling him. But he soon became a close friend of Prince Louis Bonaparte, the future Napoleon III, and of his cousin Napoléon-Jérôme, with whom the count undertook numerous study voyages. An eager follower of the Industrial Revolution in Britain, in 1852 he became a joint founder of the Crédit Foncier de France and of the Chemins de Fer Français (the French railway company) in Algeria, and with the Pereire brothers he helped to fund Haussmann's remodeling of Paris. He was a very wealthy man.

When he bought Montrésor in 1849, the estate was terribly neglected. He renovated the château—built in 1493 by Imbert de Batarnay, grandfather of Diane de Poitiers—and the grounds in the neo-Gothic style then in vogue. And in the middle of the Touraine countryside, he set about creating the romantic atmosphere of the great Polish castles of his childhood.

He hung the walls of the reception rooms with sumptuous painted fabrics—predominantly pink in the small salon, turquoise-blue in the Italian painters' salon, rich bronze in the hunt dining room. For the bedchambers, where the atmosphere was more intimate, he chose fabrics and wallpapers in harmonious shades of blue and silver, blue and gold, and green and gray, with delicate patterns of flowers, foliage, and birds. It is rare nowadays to find decorations from this period with colors that are still so fresh.

In the small salon, the eye is attracted by a large painting of *Christ and the Woman Taken in Adultery* after Veronese. The Italian painters' salon houses some of the Italian Renaissance paintings bought by the count at the sale of the collection of Cardinal Fesch, uncle of Napoleon Bonaparte: *St. Catherine of Alexandria* after Bronzino, *The Crossing of the Red Sea* by Filippino Lippi, and *Apollo and Daphne* by Bartolomeo Balducci, pupil of Botticelli.

On the first floor, Count Branicki hung the library with family portraits by Franz Xaver Winterhalter, mostly depicting his sisters and female cousins, including *Catherine Dressed à la Turque*, *Elisa and her Children*, *Princess Lubomirska*, and *The Princesses Narishkin*. *Woman in a Turban*, meanwhile, is a portrait of the beautiful and fascinating Countess Potocka, with whom the czar was so smitten that he had her husband locked up in a tower in Moscow for four long years.

Long passages densely hung with paintings lead us next to the grand salon, containing two imposing portraits of Branicki forebears, Count Franciszek Ksawery Branicki and his wife, née Aleksandra von Engelhardt.

Aleksandra was the niece of Prince Potemkin, Russian chief minister under Catherine the Great. When she was eighteen, Potemkin presented her to the czarina, whose confidante she became, and when he died he left her his entire fortune. Now immensely wealthy, she married Count Branicki and had five children with him, including the ancestor of the present owners of Montrésor.

As I study these portraits and black-and-white photographs from another era, Countess Stanislas Rey, née Marie Potocka, who now lives in the great château, explains to me (with her charming Slavic accent) how over the years Montrésor has striven to embrace, support, and shelter all those who have been forced into exile. At Montrésor they are certain to find a haven of peace, amid the warm, generous atmosphere of a genuine family home. ✑

FACING PAGE *A long passage densely hung with pictures leads to the grand salon on the first floor.* RIGHT *An eighteenth-century watercolor of the château (top), and a view of the medieval ramparts on which Imbert de Batarnay built the Renaissance château (bottom).*

AT MONTRÉSOR, EVERYONE COMMANDS AND NO ONE OBEYS.
NAPOLÉON-JÉRÔME BONAPARTE

LEFT *A service in Bohemian crystal.*
ABOVE *The walls of the hunt dining room are hung with bronze fabric and decorated with a heraldic frieze, a bust of Constantin Branicki, and hunting trophies including a stag's head, a boar's head, and a Polish wolf.*
FACING PAGE *The walls of the passage leading to the dining room bristle with Count Xavier Branicki's hunting trophies, including the stuffed heads of two wolves killed at Montrésor in 1895.*

AT THE AGE OF EIGHTEEN, THE BEAUTIFUL ALEKSANDRA, NIECE OF PRINCE POTEMKIN AND FUTURE COUNTESS BRANICKA, WAS ONE OF CATHERINE THE GREAT'S CLOSEST CONFIDANTES.

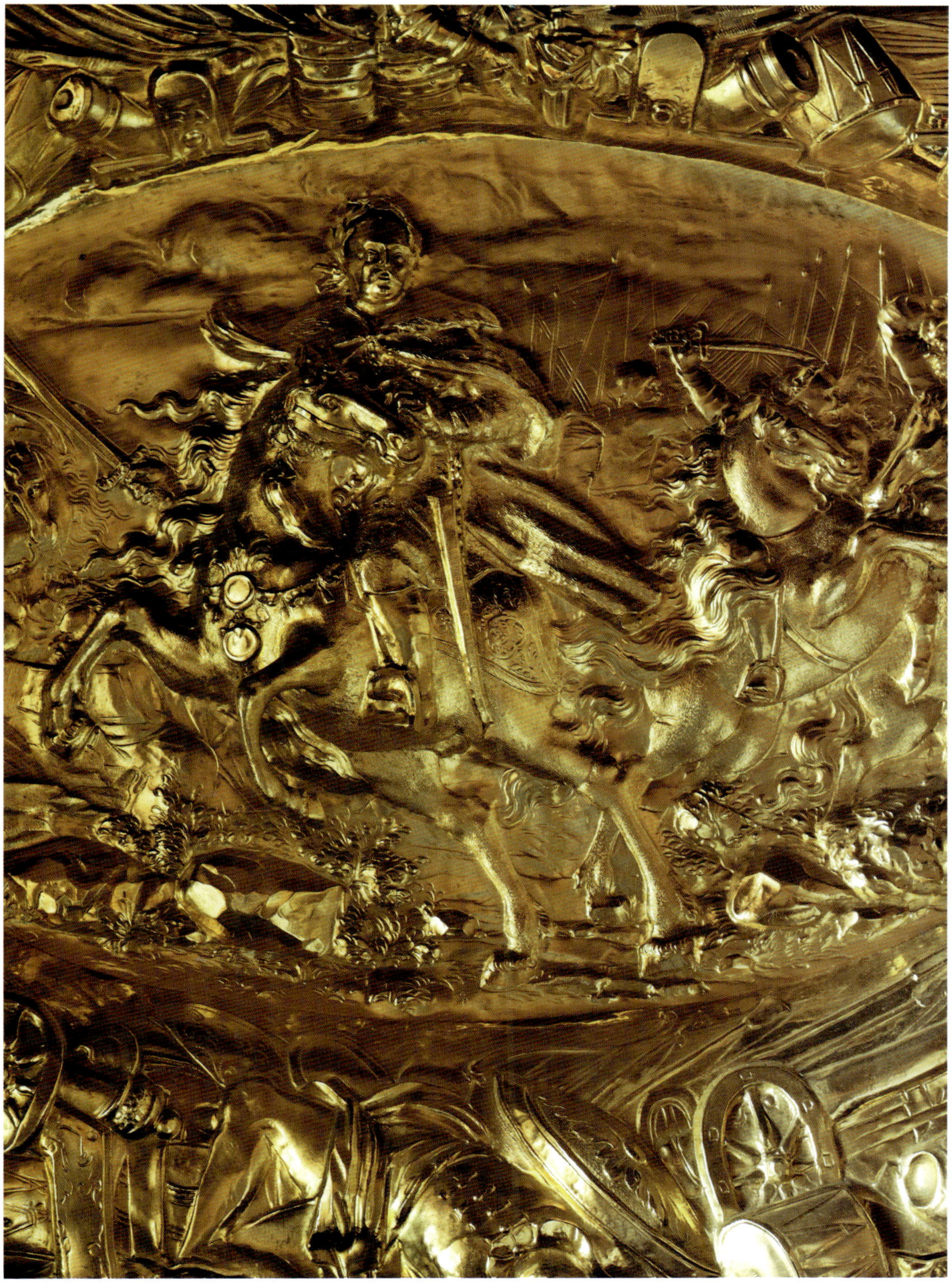

FACING PAGE *The windows in the small paneled cabinet are embellished with family crests.*
ABOVE *A portrait of Aleksandra von Engelhardt, who married Count Franciszek Ksawery Branicki, hangs in the grand salon on the first floor. Niece of Prince Potemkin, she became one of Catherine the Great's closest confidantes when she was just eighteen. Her five children with the count included Ladislas, ancestor of the present owners of Montrésor.*
RIGHT *A magnificent vermeil charger with high-relief decoration depicting the Polish king John III Sobieski, victor over the Ottoman Turks at the Battle of Vienna in 1683.*

ON HIS COUNTRY ESTATE, COUNT XAVIER BRANICKI RECREATED THE ROMANTIC ATMOSPHERE OF THE GREAT POLISH DOMAINS OF HIS CHILDHOOD.

FACING PAGE *An oriental saddle pommel encrusted with semi-precious stones.*
RIGHT *A historic engraving of the baroque Wilanów Palace near Warsaw, the Polish seat of the House of Branicki.*
BELOW *Watercolor by Georges Buisson of Count Nicolas Potocki, who was famous for his magnificent horses and carriages.*

ONE OF THOSE HOUSES WHERE EVERY SITTING ROOM IS LIKE
A CABINET OF GREENERY, AND EVERY BEDROOM IS LINED EITHER
WITH ROSES FROM THE GARDEN OR BIRDS FROM THE TREES,
WHICH JOIN YOU AND KEEP YOU COMPANY. MARCEL PROUST, *Time Regained*

LEFT St. Catherine of Alexandria *after Bronzino.*
ABOVE *Detail of the library curtains, showing their broad tapestry inserts.*
FACING PAGE *Displayed in the Italian painters' salon, its walls hung with a nineteenth-century painted fabric in a floral design, are some of the Italian Renaissance paintings from the collection of Cardinal Fesch, uncle of Napoleon Bonaparte. The twenty-three paintings bought in 1845 by Count Xavier Branicki include* Apollo and Daphne *by Bartolomeo Balducci, pupil of Botticelli.*

FACING PAGE *The remarkable Cuban mahogany spiral staircase in the small salon was an exhibit at the 1855 Exposition Universelle.*
BELOW *The large painting of* Christ and the Woman Taken in Adultery *after Veronese came from Prince Napoleon's collection at the Palais-Royal. On the right-hand wall is a portrait of Princess Sapiéha painted by Madame Vigée-Lebrun in St. Petersburg.*

ABOVE AND FACING PAGE *In the library, Count Xavier Branicki brought together family portraits, consisting principally of late nineteenth-century portraits by Winterhalter of his sisters and female cousins, notably* Catherine [his sister] Dressed à la Turque *(above),* Catherine in a White Gown *(facing page, right) and* Elisa and her Children *(facing page, left). On the easel is an interior view of Countess Branicka's Paris salon on rue de Penthièvre, painted by the countess herself. The walls are hung with a nineteenth-century fabric painted in a floral pattern.*
RIGHT *The romantic Countess Potocka, painted in a red-and-white turban by Heinrich Hollpein in 1845; in the medallions above are portraits of the Princesses Narishkin.*

234 PRIVATE HOUSES OF FRANCE: LIVING WITH HISTORY

FACING PAGE *The pink bedroom, with its pretty* lit à la polonaise, *epitomizes the romanticism of Montrésor.* RIGHT *A crystal "night service" engraved with a decoration of grapevines, and (below) a family photograph.*

BELOW AND FACING PAGE *Sunrise at Montrésor reveals the last of the season's flowers powdered with frost. Their petals echo the wonderfully fresh colors of the wallpaper in one of the bedchambers (facing page). These exquisite wallpapers, of a quality, richness, and delicacy that would be impossible to find today, are now one of Montrésor's many attractions.*

FACING PAGE *A remarkable mid nineteenth-century wallpaper patterned in gold and silver on a blue ground, highly characteristic of fashions in taste at the time when Count Branicki completed the interior decorations at Montrésor.*
BELOW *The Renaissance château and its romantic gardens glimpsed from a window in one of the outbuildings.*

THERE IS NOT A TREE, NOT A CLUMP OF PINKS, NOT A CUSHION OF MOSS THAT IS NOT ENGRAVED ON OUR SOUL AS THOUGH IT WERE PART OF IT! THIS CORNER OF LAND SEEMS VAST TO US, SO MANY OBJECTS AND MEMORIES DOES IT CONTAIN IN SO CONFINED A SPACE. ALPHONSE DE LAMARTINE, *Milly*

LEFT AND ABOVE *The little library on the ground floor, and Laure's great-aunt Colombe.*
FACING PAGE *In this hôtel particulier in the Marais, home to Laure, a painter, you feel you are in the privacy of a real family home, filled with life and character.*

FAMILY
MEMORIES IN THE MARAIS

FACING PAGE *Landscapes, portraits, and still lifes by Laure mingle happily with older works. The half-open door offers a glimpse of her primrose-yellow bedroom, with her portrait of her daughter.*

When you enter this *hôtel particulier* hidden away at the end of a courtyard in the Marais, you immediately feel you are in a proper family home, filled with life and memories. Laure, who greets me, is the direct descendant of all the inhabitants of this house since the eighteenth century. These are the people who have given this beautiful house not only its character but also its soul—the soul of a house that is truly "lived in."

Laure takes me straight up to the first floor, whisking me quickly through the ground floor—formerly the reserve of kitchens and store rooms—and up the sweeping main staircase, of stone construction with a magnificent wrought-iron balustrade. My eye is immediately drawn to an array of paintings displayed on a tomato-red wall—a juxtaposition of contrasting colors that infuses the space with a cheerful atmosphere. One door opens into Laure's bedroom, painted primrose yellow, another into the large salon, flooded with light.

My curiosity is piqued by a little door cut discreetly into the paneling beside the fireplace. Laure opens it to reveal a tiny room filled with family photographs, letters, and archives. This is where she comes to write, where she conjures up all her memories, real or reinvented, and hones her writing to give life to her familiar characters. One day, by chance, she opened one of the many drawers to discover the private diary of her paternal grandmother, the lovely Olympe. This was the journal to which Olympe consigned the hopes and joys of a young girl at the end of the nineteenth century. Leafing through its pages, I have the sensation of capturing, for that fleeting moment, the authentic soul of this house. And above all its character.

We are in 1887. Olympe, Laure's grandmother, is just fifteen. She writes: "It seemed that every morning a new era was opening up for me, with all my dreams of freedom and adventure, with my veins filled not with blood but with liquid silver.... My character is like an iron rod, rather than bend I shall break.... I want to love with a passion, I shall be a woman of burning ardor for the man who can master me, but when?" And again: "Why was I born a woman? Freedom, ambition, independence, the passions, a taste for strenuous exercise, science, studies—all this is for men, not for women!" Passionately in love from the age of sixteen with a man who was magnificent but penniless, she hid her torment behind a radiant smile. She dazzled with her charm and her laughter; she was delightful but turned down all the suitors who were introduced to her, determined to remain faithful to the man she loved. In the end she married him, fifteen years later, flying in the face of her family's refusal to accept him and society's disapproval. But this great love, so long awaited, was to be tragically short-lived: on June 16, 1915 he was killed in the trenches, leaving Olympe inconsolable.

Reading between the lines of her diary, the portrait emerges of another person who lived here, her sister, "*la belle* Colombe." A great beauty admired by all, Colombe was unmoved by all the adulation she received, declaring that she just wanted to die. Olympe noted in her diary: "Our arrival at the ball was a tremendous success, but Colombe was the only one who existed, and Lord was she lovely! Everyone had eyes only for her. This is what beauty, true beauty, can do. She is a wonder, a goddess, a queen!" In the dining room is a portrait of this young girl, with a gentle and melancholy air, her hair swept up into bouffant fashion of the Belle Époque. Tilting her head with a sad, distant smile, she already seems far removed from the world she would leave at the age of just twenty-five.

Laure, who is fortunate enough to live in the magnificent house today, has devoted her whole life to her art. Her paintings, mostly portraits and still lifes, cover the walls. Her bright yellow bedroom, with its glorious Louis XVI canopy bed, seems to be filled with high spirits and

energy, perfectly encapsulating her love of vibrant contrasts. The bathroom—which used to be the pantry in the days when the kitchen was on the ground floor—is a delicate combination of mahogany, crystal, opaline, and vintage linen.

Laure invites me into her private world next: her studio, overlooking the courtyard. A place of calm and tranquility, lit by a cool wintry light. This is where she finds the quiet and concentration she needs for her work. This is where she can hone her eye and perfect her art. In her youth, she too was feted and admired. She too used to love to go to balls—the "Bal des Têtes," the "Bal des Bijoux," the balls thrown by Baron Alexis de Redé, and more. She too loved couture gowns by Balmain, Lanvin, and Dior. Nowadays she loves nothing better than to work in her studio in silence. Surrounded by her portraits, and by her vivid paints that she mixes with such dexterity, she is full of vitality and enthusiasm. She is one of those women of sturdy, mettlesome character who never lose heart. She faces up to the vicissitudes of life, greeting all its surprises, however strange or serious, with a peal of laughter.

LEFT *An art deco vase in emerald green pâte de verre.*
FACING PAGE AND PAGES 248–49 *The large salon looking out over the garden, with its elegant eighteenth-century paneling. Above the lacquer and gilt wood temple flowers hangs a self-portrait by Laure.*

TIME ERASES ALL; IT CANNOT DIM EYES, WHETHER PALE OR STARRY OR CLEAR.

MARCEL PROUST, "I Often Contemplate the Sky of My Memory"

FACING PAGE *A concave door let into the paneling leads into the tiny room that Laure has turned into her study. Surrounded by letters, photographs, and family archives, this is where she writes her memoirs.*
ABOVE *A photograph of Laure's maternal grandparents taken in the 1900s.*
RIGHT *Olympe, Laure's paternal grandmother, a woman of character, painted by Helleu in a town costume and feather hat. In the family archives Laure found her private diary, to which she confided her hopes and passions in the late nineteenth century.*

FAMILY MEMORIES IN THE MARAIS

HOUSES MAKE TREMENDOUS HIDING PLACES FOR PUTTING REAL LIFE INTO STORAGE. FRANÇOIS NOURISSIER, *La Maison Mélancolie*

ABOVE AND RIGHT *A pretty sketchbook bound in red morocco.*
FACING PAGE *Laure in around 1960, in a Lanvin gown and with her hair dressed by Alexandre.*

LEFT, ABOVE, AND FACING PAGE *In the sea-green dining room, surrounded by antique engravings, hangs a portrait of Olympe's sister: the wistful Colombe, who died of melancholy at twenty-five.*

A METAPHORICAL TEMPTATION RUNS THROUGH MY HEAD: TO GIVE
EXPRESSION TO THIS INTUITIVE FEELING THAT THE HOUSE IS A LANGUAGE.
FRANÇOIS NOURISSIER, *La Maison Mélancolie*

FACING PAGE *A collection of crystal decanter stoppers glitters in the light.*
RIGHT AND BELOW *Portrait of Laure's grandfather, and detail of an engraved monogram on a crystal plate.*
PAGES 258 AND 259 *Laure's cheerful bedroom, with its lit à la polonaise hung with raspberry-and-green-striped taffeta and its primrose-yellow walls. Near the window hangs one of her many portraits of her daughter and granddaughters.*

LEFT, ABOVE, AND FACING PAGE *The old pantry, now a bathroom, makes a charming mahogany-paneled backdrop for a collection of crystal boxes and bottles. Old family photographs evoke memories going back generations.*
PAGES 262 AND 263 *The second-floor enfilade.*

BELOW AND FACING PAGE *Laure paints her portraits and landscapes in her studio on the ground floor, where she finds the concentration she needs for her art. Some years ago, she even painted my portrait (below).*

LEFT *The stone staircase in the magnificent Hôtel Lambert, built by Louis Le Vau in 1640 on the tip of the Île Saint-Louis for the financier Jean-Baptiste Lambert, adviser and secretary to the king.*
ABOVE *Baroness Guy de Rothschild with another guest at the Bal Oriental given by Alexis de Redé in 1969.*
FACING PAGE *A detail of the painted decorations by Eustache Le Sueur in the Galerie d'Hercule.*

LUNCH
WITH ALEXIS DE REDÉ

That night in July 2013, gazing at the terrible images of the Hôtel Lambert engulfed in flames, my thoughts went back to the sunny day when Alexis de Redé had been kind enough to invite me to lunch in what I believe to be one of the most beautiful *hôtels particuliers* in Paris.

I see myself ten years earlier, climbing the imposing stone staircase up to the first floor. I stop for a moment in the doorway of the magnificent Galerie d'Hercule to admire the ceilings painted by Charles Le Brun before he decorated the Hall of Mirrors at Versailles. Awe-struck by the splendor of the decorations, dazzled by the light shimmering on the parquet floors, I felt as though I were in some great galleon moored on the banks of the Seine.

We drank a glass of champagne beside the majestic mahogany bookcase made by Georges Geffroy, the distinguished interior decorator of the post-war period. I admire its stucco columns, painted to look like lapis lazuli, the magnificent leather-bound volumes, and the collection of bronzes and curios, including a remarkable shagreen-sheathed astronomical telescope.

We crossed the gilded grand salon with its wealth of painted grisaille decorations by Eustache Le Sueur. The room was lit by a rock crystal chandelier, and everywhere there were orchids, adding a note of gaiety to the majesty and lyricism of that extraordinary space.

It was in the Salon des Muses that Alexis liked to welcome his guests for lunch. Arranged in the center of a small round table was a bouquet of his favourite roses, carefully spritzed by the maître d'hôtel before our arrival so that they looked as though they were spangled with dew. It was this subtle attention to detail that captured the essence of this house, which seemed—wherever you looked—to have been touched by magic.

I remember the miraculous *soufflés aux truffes*, the *langoustines flambées*, and an exquisite dessert with a hint of mandarin. Alexis devoted as much care to the pleasures of the table as he did to art: every detail of his surroundings reflected a *savoir vivre* raised to the level of a fine art.

I think also of how fortunate I was that day to revisit the famous Cabinet des Bains—the small attic room that he used as a dressing room—painted by Eustache Le Sueur in the seventeenth century. The ceiling, painted with a gold trelliswork design of flowers and foliage against a ravishing blue sky, was enchanting. Cavorting on all sides were mythological figures on a watery theme, river gods, goddesses trailing undulating trains of seaweed, unicorns with fish tails, seahorses, shells, and branches of red coral. This was the incomparable décor that was destroyed by fire on the night of July 10, 2013.

Next door to it lay the room where Alexis slept. For its silver-blue tent-like decorations he had drawn inspiration, with the help of the interior designer Victor Grandpierre, from the bedchamber of the Comte d'Artois at Bagatelle. Bundled lances in gilt bronze supported the tent and lent the room a surprisingly military air. Leaving these private rooms behind, I walked down the long passage that retained the stamp of the era of the Princes Czartoryski, the famous Polish noblemen who bought the Hôtel Lambert in the 1830s, on the advice of Eugène Delacroix. It was they who turned it into a great center of nineteenth-century Polish politics and culture, frequented by Chopin among others. And it was from the Czartoryski family that from 1947 Alexis de Redé rented the piano nobile of the Hôtel Lambert.

Before finding himself suddenly alone in the world, Alexis de Redé had enjoyed a pampered and luxurious childhood in Switzerland, living in sixteen rooms of the grand Hôtel Dolder in Zurich with his mother, brother, and sister. It was a carefree, happy time. But when he was nine, in 1931, his mother died of leukemia. Sent to the famous Swiss boarding school

PAGES 268–69 *The Galerie d'Hercule flooded with afternoon sunlight. The famous ceiling painted around 1655 by Charles Le Brun features the* Labors of Hercules. *The three apsidal windows offer spectacular views over the Seine. This was the setting for some of the twentieth century's most celebrated balls and parties.*
FACING PAGE *Portrait of Baron Alexis de Redé in the library at the Hôtel Lambert, c.1950. This aesthete par excellence occupied the piano nobile for nearly sixty years, transforming it into a timeless, fairy-tale setting of palatial splendor.*

the Institut Le Rosey, he was told a few years later that his father was ruined and had killed himself. Aged just seventeen, he found himself virtually alone in the world, in uncertain times, knowing that his Jewish roots on his mother's side placed him in danger. He left for America, where he worked for an antique dealer for a while before meeting Arturo Lopez Willshaw, the renowned Chilean-born art collector and connoisseur.

Together they set off for Paris, where in 1947 Victor Grandpierre mentioned to them that the first floor of the Hôtel Lambert, still in the possession of the Princes Czartoryski, was available to rent. Alexis fell under the building's spell, and decided to make it his home forever. With the help of Arturo Lopez and the Monuments Historiques, he coaxed the woefully dilapidated rooms back to all their former glory, restoring the painted decorations, the Galerie d'Hercule, and the salons, and decorating them with an outstanding collection of furniture and objets d'art. On his death in 1962, Arturo Lopez bequeathed him his half of their collection.

Alexis de Redé lived in the Hôtel Lambert for nearly sixty years. When Baron and Baroness Guy de Rothschild bought the building in 1975, it was agreed that he would remain there for the rest of his days. He died on July 8, 2004. From childhood he had dreamed of a golden world, and this was what he had found in his timeless palace.

PAGES 272–73 *The inner courtyard of the Hôtel Lambert with its pair of white elephants for the Bal Oriental given by Alexis de Redé on December 5, 1969.*
ABOVE, LEFT *Jacqueline Delubac, third wife of Sacha Guitry, with Victor Grandpierre (right), the interior designer who worked at the Hôtel Lambert, and Alexis de Redé in the 1950s.*
BELOW, LEFT *Baron and Baroness Guy de Rothschild with Alexis de Redé (right) in the late 1970s.*

Alexis de Redé lived in complete symbiosis with this magical place, which he had transformed into a palace worthy of the *Thousand and One Nights*. In the years after the war he gave unforgettable balls and parties there. The magnificent Bal des Têtes in 1956 was an extraordinary success. His friend Lilia Ralli had suggested that a young assistant working with Christian Dior, one Yves Mathieu-Saint-Laurent, might design the twenty extravagant coiffures. Dinners and balls succeeded one another in the Galerie d'Hercule, culminating in the legendary Bal Oriental on December 5, 1969, one of the most spectacular society occasions of the twentieth century.

Alexis de Redé was an aesthete, a prince of elegance. Quiet and melancholic by temperament, he was nocturnal by nature, and loved nothing more than to be surrounded by his rare books, his sumptuous furniture, and all his other magnificent pieces. Together they embodied to perfection the *art de vivre*—and perhaps brought him just a little bit closer to his own paradise lost. ✎

RIGHT *In the library, some of Alexis de Redé's collection of bronze and marble figures, morocco-bound boxes, and a superb telescope in its shagreen case.*

I LOVE THOSE WHO YEARN FOR THE IMPOSSIBLE. GOETHE, *Faust, Part Two, The Lower Peneios*

FACING PAGE *The famous bookcase designed by Georges Geffroy—a highly influential interior designer in post-war Paris—in 1948, with its faux lapis lazuli stucco columns and its collection of armorial bindings.*
ABOVE *Design by Princess Ghislaine de Polignac for Alexis de Redé's costume as Ludwig II of Bavaria for the memorable Bal d'Hiver given by the Baronne de Cabrol at the Palais des Glaces in 1954.*
RIGHT *Ostrich egg decorated by Alexandre Serebriakoff. The window pierced in the shell reveals a view of the Hôtel Lambert painted on the inner surface of the shell.*

LUNCH WITH ALEXIS DE REDÉ

BENEATH THE REAL WORLD THERE EXISTS AN IDEAL WORLD, WHICH REVEALS ITSELF IN ALL ITS SPLENDOR TO THOSE WHOM GRAVE MEDITATIONS HAVE ACCUSTOMED TO SEEING MORE IN THINGS THAN MERE OBJECTS. VICTOR HUGO, Preface to *Odes et Ballades*

LEFT AND FACING PAGE *The library with its famous silver furniture in Regency style, and the enfilade of rooms overlooking the garden.* ABOVE *A bronze figure of a pugilist, in bronze with a brown patina, silhouetted against the window.*

"I LOVE EVERY STONE OF THIS MAGNIFICENT PLACE.
RESTORING AND PRESERVING IT HAS BEEN MY LIFE."
ALEXIS DE REDÉ

FACING PAGE *The gilded grand salon with its magnificent grisaille decorations by Eustache Le Sueur.* ABOVE AND RIGHT *A period photograph of the salon, and a lovely eighteenth-century terra-cotta bust of a girl by Clodion.*

NO EXPLANATION IN WORDS CAN EVER TAKE THE PLACE OF CONTEMPLATION. ANTOINE DE SAINT-EXUPÉRY, *Pilote de Guerre*

ABOVE AND FACING PAGE *Alexis de Redé's Japanese lacquer bureau plat in the grand salon overlooking the garden. Arranged on the leather top with gold tooling are precious objets including a lyre, cases and boxes, and a box of knives with delicate eighteenth-century porcelain handles. A charming Italian eighteenth-century polychrome wooden figure of a commedia dell'arte acrobat balances on one foot.*

FACING PAGE *The fireplace in the gilded grand salon, with its grand mirrors that create a mise en abyme of the room's superb gray-and-gold boiseries.* ABOVE AND RIGHT *Details of a gilt bronze clock and a rock crystal pendant.*

"I HAVE NO DINING ROOM: I SET A TABLE." ALEXIS DE REDÉ

FACING PAGE, ABOVE, AND RIGHT
For intimate lunches, Alexis de Redé liked to receive his guests in the Salon des Muses, where a table was always decorated with a bouquet of his favorite roses. The dishes prepared by the chef were invariably exquisite.

ABOVE AND LEFT *Detail of a gilt bronze firedog, and a collection of delicate Bohemian crystal glasses.*
FACING PAGE *The remarkable Salon des Muses, decorated by Le Sueur.*

MAGICAL MOMENTS THAT LINGER FOREVER IN THE MEMORY.

FACING PAGE *This superlative André-Charles Boulle secretaire in the Salon des Muses, decorated by Le Sueur, is one of only three known examples; one used to be at Knole House, childhood home of Vita Sackville-West, and the other is now in Buckingham Palace.*

LEFT *Sketch for a headdress by Yves Saint Laurent for the Bal des Têtes given by Alexis de Redé in 1957.*
ABOVE AND RIGHT *Guests arriving for a ball at the Hôtel Lambert in 1967, including (clockwise from top left) Monsieur and Madame Bernard Lanvin; Baron and Baroness Alain de Rothschild and Madame Brignone; Alexis de Redé welcoming his guests; and the Comtesse de Larozière with a friend.*

FACING PAGE *Alexis de Redé's attic bedroom, with its silver-blue tent décor, was designed by Victor Grandpierre after the bedchamber of the Comte d'Artois at Bagatelle.*
BELOW *Drawing in pen and gray ink showing the Galerie d'Hercule in the eighteenth century.*

TO FIND AND THEN TO LOSE ONESELF, IN COUNTRIES, IN TIMES, FLOATING LIKE THE SILENCE OF ARPEGGIOS FROM UNHEARD PIANOS. ALBERT SAMAIN, *Confins*

BELOW AND FACING PAGE *The famous Cabinet des Bains was completely destroyed in the fire of July 2013. The enchanting ceiling decorations, painted by Eustache le Sueur, the "French Raphael," between 1652 and 1655, depicted aquatic and mythological figures including sea gods, seaweed, shells, arabesques, putti, and coral branches. On the commode (below) stands a seventeenth-century mother-of-pearl ewer and basin from the Dutch East Indies (detail, below, right).*

ACKNOWLEDGMENTS

I am grateful to all the owners of these magnificent houses for welcoming me
so generously into the privacy of their homes. To experience the beauty of these places
and to see them so filled with life has been both a joy and a tonic.
Thank you to Francis Hammond for his magnificent photographs.
Thank you to Christina Vervitsioti-Missoffe for her photographs, taken in 2002,
of a delightful lunch with Alexis de Redé at the Hôtel Lambert.
Thank you to Victor Skrebneski for his wonderful portrait of Hubert de Givenchy.
Thank you to Count Hervé d'Andigné for his hunting expertise and for his fascinating
book *Voix dans Voies*, published by Éditions de la Croix du Loup.
Thank you to my sister France de Nicolay-Anthonioz for her help, invariably both wise and valuable.
Thank you to Art Digital Studio—Philippe Grandperrin, Louis Blancard,
Jean-Yves and Nicolas Dubois—and to Marina Gadonneix for their photographs.
Thank you to my editor Suzanne Tise-Isoré, director of the Style & Design Collection,
whose enthusiasm and Franco-American culture have made our collaboration so delightful.
Thank you to Bernard Lagacé, the talented designer of this book,
with whom it is always such a pleasure to work.
Thank you to Frédérique Popet, Sarah Rozelle, and Lucie Lurton.
Thank you to Philippine de Lanquesaint and to Véronique Benitah for their assistance.

PHOTOGRAPHIC CREDITS

t: top, b: bottom, l: left, r: right
All photographs in this book were taken by Francis Hammond
with the exception of the following:
p. 2: © Christina Vervitsioti-Missoffe; p. 8: © musée des Beaux-Arts de Dijon/François Jay;
pp. 31tl, 31bl, and 34b: private collection; p. 37r: © Succession J.-C. Fourneau; p. 68l:
© Christiane de Nicolay-Mazery; pp. 79b, 102, and 120br: private collection; p. 124r: © RMN-Grand Palais
(domaine de Chantilly)/René-Gabriel Ojéda; p. 148r: private collection; p. 151: © Christian Bérard/Adagp,
Paris 2014; p. 153l: private collection; pp. 153r and 158: © Marina Gadonneix; p. 159l: © Christian Bérard/
Adagp, Paris 2014; p. 159r: © Roger Schall/Pictures Inc./Time Life Pictures/Getty Images;
p. 160l: © Marina Gadonneix; p. 160r: © Étienne-Adrien Drian/Adagp, Paris, 2014; p. 161: © Marina
Gadonneix; p. 165: © Victor Skrebneski; p. 168t: © Rue des Archives/AGIP; pp. 168b, 209, 212l, and 215tr:
private collection; p. 227l: © Fine Art Images/Heritage Images/Scala, Florence, 2014; pp. 229, 237br, 242r,
251, and 253: private collection; p. 266l: © Christina Vervitsioti-Missoffe; p. 266r: private collection; p. 267:
© Art Digital Studio; pp. 268 and 269: © Christina Vervitsioti-Missoffe; pp. 271–274: private collection;
p. 275: © Art Digital Studio; p. 276: © Christina Vervitsioti-Missoffe; p. 277l: private collection;
p. 277r: © Art Digital Studio; p. 278l: © Christina Vervitsioti-Missoffe; p. 278r: © Art Digital Studio;
pp. 279 and 280: © Christina Vervitsioti-Missoffe; p. 281l: private collection; pp. 281r–285: © Art Digital
Studio; pp. 286 and 287l: © Christina Vervitsioti-Missoffe; pp. 287r, 288, and 289: © Art Digital Studio;
p. 290: © Christina Vervitsioti-Missoffe; p. 291bl: Fondation Pierre Bergé-Yves Saint Laurent Archives;
p. 291 (other photographs): private collection; pp. 292–299: © Art Digital Studio.

FACING PAGE *Detail from the ceiling of the Cabinet des
Bains, showing its delicate tracery of wrought ironwork
intertwined with boughs of flowering jasmine.*